MIN

How to Live a Happy Minimalist Life

Marc Gillespie

CONTENTS

"The secret of happiness, you see, is not found in seeking more, but in developing the capacity to enjoy less"

Socrates

Introduction

In this book, we'll discuss minimalism as well as the decluttering (both physical and mental) that follows. I'm not sure which comes first. Do you decide to become a minimalist first, then start to declutter, or do you decide to become a minimalist first, then start to declutter? Like I said: I'm not sure. I suppose it functions both ways. For me, I believe it began with decluttering before evolving into a minimalist lifestyle over time. It has wonderful side effects as well, such a boost in happiness, clarity, and time.

Even though I didn't realise it for a very long time, my inner minimalism was always strong.

I've always had the impression that having less stuff makes me happier. According to my buddy Martin, who lived with me in Germany for more than seven years in the 1990s, my apartment usually appeared as though I had either moved in or was getting ready to leave.

A couch, a TV, a DVD player, a stereo, two chairs, a small table, an office chair, a cabinet, two seats, a PlayStation, and a desk. There it was. It was fantastic!

I didn't have a job nine years ago. Today, in the charming city of Budapest, one of the liveliest capitals in Europe, I am living the life of my dreams. Writing novels, napping, taking long walks, travelling, and occasionally watching Netflix are some of the things I enjoy doing the most. I still have time to work 7 to 8 hour days. Actually, four or five hour days are more common at the present.

Why did I arrive there? Good habits, minimalism and decluttering, perseverance, and hard work.

This book is unsuitable for you if you are looking for a quick-rich scheme or urgent financial assistance. Success takes time, just like good things.

It won't be simple, but it will get simpler as you go.

Eliminating the superfluous and concentrating on the essential is what minimalism entails. You will discover joy, fulfilment, and freedom if you commit to this way of living.

As with any changes, simplicity can be achieved. small steps. These modest changes will eventually lead to significant change. The key phrase is daily. Incremental. Changes.

All change begins with the decision to bring about change, and this decision needs to be immediately followed by action. It needs to be followed up with a positive action step. and another one follows. And yet another

I must disappoint you if you were hoping for any fantastic new insights on the issue of minimalism and decluttering. They are not included in this book. What you will discover is a collection of ideas from numerous other books on minimalism and decluttering that I utilised in my own life and that significantly improved, facilitated, and improved my quality of life.

Despite its title, this is not a novel about happiness. It is a book on decluttering and simplicity. However, I really believe that if you implement the exercises and ideas from this book into your life (the more, the better), you will improve your happiness as you go.

This book won't be very long. Although you could assume the contrary after reading this introduction. I won't spend 50 pages explaining to you how to clean your house. I'll try to persuade you to take action. I suggest Steve (S.J.) Scott and Barrie Davenport's book 10-Minute Declutter if you need more details on decluttering, such as shopping lists and a description of cleaning each area and each drawer separately. They go into great depth about how you can proceed.

I only brought one duffel bag to Barcelona in 2003. I already required three duffle bags when I relocated for the second time. However, moving my belongings just required one taxi ride. When we relocated again in 2011 when I met my (now ex-) wife, we needed a small vehicle and three trips to carry our belongings.

In 2018, I acted alone once more. I used Mari Kondo's KonMari Method above everything else to get rid of more than half of my belongings because I was relocating on a boat. But I also applied techniques I learned from the minimalists, Joshua Becker's Simplify, Steve (S.J.) Scott and Barrie Davenport's book 10-Minute Declutter, and numerous blog articles. In addition to moving to the boat because I've always wanted to live on one, I did it to make myself get go of a lot of my belongings. I had already completely adopted the maxim "less is more."

I relocated once more in 2020. This time, I travelled by plane to the island of Malta. I was forced to throw even more things away at this point. Unexpectedly, I was back to carrying just a huge and a little suitcase. Moving is therefore actually one of the finest ways to declutter and get rid of things. When I was waiting for my flight to the lovely island where I would be relocating in Frankfurt, I had to smile. People who were travelling for two or three weeks had more luggage than I did as I stood there with just one large and one little suitcase with everything I owned.

I regrettably had to leave the stunning island of Malta sooner than I had hoped, so I relocated once more. One suitcase was supplied to me, and I only brought one with me (sendmybag.com shipped it to my place in the centre of Budapest within 24 hours). There it was. One and a half suitcases can hold everything I own. By the time I relocate once again in the future, I'll probably have it down to one.

Anyway, enough about my history of relocating. Above all, reading the aforementioned books and putting their advice into practise were crucial. The same will take place with you. This book will entertain you even if you merely read it, or at least that's my hope. Some of the information presented here could advance your life if you put it into practise.

Perhaps you'll experience greater happiness than ever before or a sense of freedom you've never experienced before. I'm not sure. You have the choice.

Living a minimalist lifestyle does not require you to have nothing, a set quantity of possessions, or for everything to fit into a single suitcase. It implies that you live more intentionally and simply. In a furnished 120 square metre (1300 square foot) apartment, I lived simply. This didn't imply that I had abandoned minimalism. It indicates that I was still quite careful about my purchases. I kept my apartment tidy. I did, however, make a mistake. I rented the apartment assuming I'd have a lot of guests and require a lot of space. Well, I was by myself a lot of the time because of the Pandemic. I made another downsizing in Budapest. I currently live in a 65 square metre apartment, which is still more than big enough for one person and two people. The most crucial thing is to maintain it clutter-free since both physical and mental clutter diverts my attention from what is truly important.

Let me be clear about something before I start to look like one of Klaus Schwab's agents (that's the moron who predicted that by 2030, "you'll own nothing and will be happy"). I own almost nothing, and I'm extremely happy about it, but it was MY CHOICE, not something some evil millionaire and his stooges imposed onto me. And that difference is MASSIVE.

This book is not long. I believed that writing a 200-page book on minimalism would be excessive. Less can be more.

I won't claim to have created a brand-new system or give it a catchy name. I just put into practise what Marie Kondo and other writers who have written excellent books about organising systems teach. You ought to read these as well. However, you might not need to if you APPLY what you learn in this book.

Going room by room seems to make the decluttering process go more smoothly for me. I currently have the benefit of moving into a furnished apartment and having almost nothing, so my task is a little bit different because I've already done the decluttering. Therefore, "don't gather too much stuff" is not my motto.

But even though it might begin with it, this is about more than just getting rid of useless items. You'll likely get more adept at making decisions over time and let go of unneeded emotions, unneeded restricting beliefs, unpleasant relationships, and unreliable business partners. The true miracle is that.

Your life will become much simpler as your mind becomes more clear. Most likely, you won't ever want to return to your former habits. And time, oh my, you'll have so much more of it once you eliminate the distractions.

Enough said!

Let's start the fun ride.

WHAT IS MINIMALISM?

With minimalism, you have options. about wiser decisions. It's about keeping only what is really required and getting rid of everything else. In order to get more out of the things we choose to say "Yes" to, it's equally important to choose to say "No" to many other things.

It involves accepting the tenets of "quality over quantity" and "less is more." However, what matters most is how minimal you feel comfortable and content with being. No regulations exist. To me, minimalism can mean something completely different than to you. There isn't a method that works for everyone. While some minimalists have just 100, 50, or even fewer things, my aim when becoming a minimalist was to get rid of everything I didn't actually need. I was eventually able to pack everything I owned into a single large suitcase as a result of this method. In any case, you may live a minimalist lifestyle in a 2000 square foot apartment by keeping only what is required and getting rid of everything else.

Getting things done is not the point of minimalism. It's about doing the necessary tasks. the crucial elements. what motivates you to move forward. the activities that advance you toward your objectives. It's not about gathering things. Spoiler alert: Despite what billions of dollars in advertising spend trying to convince you of, having more will not make you happier. Eliminating unnecessary items allows one to focus on what is truly important. A fantastic byproduct of simplicity is the potential to eliminate drama along with the clutter.

At its best, minimalism will improve your relationships, give your life new purpose, meaning, and emotions, as well as more time, money, and joy. Ideally, nothing will alter. So why not try it out? Based on my personal experiences, I'll explain how I came to embrace minimalism and how doing so has improved my sense of clarity, focus, and happiness. When that happens, you'll be ready to use it as you choose.

My intention is to give you routines and resources that will help you achieve the same clarity and contentment while getting rid of all the extraneous things in your life. You must clear your life of any clutter, both physical and mental, that keeps you from focusing on what matters most.

Nothing will ever be the same again once you adopt the minimalist mindset.

CULTIVATING A MINIMALIST MINDSET

Watching less TV is undoubtedly a part of becoming a minimalist. When you are constantly being urged to buy more by tens of thousands of advertisements, it is much harder to declutter and get rid of things.

Ads can be found everywhere these days, including on smartphones. Therefore, by wanting less, you go against the flow of a culture that constantly encourages us to desire more.

I'm not sure if I stopped falling for it because I became a minimalist or because I developed strong self-esteem and self-confidence. I no longer have the emotional emptiness that I used to try to fill by buying constantly. I feel comfortable in a T-shirt with no brand. (However, I must admit that I own a tonne of Nike T-shirts. I adore their tagline.)

Anyways. Your approach to life will strengthen the process, in my opinion. You keep asking yourself, "Is this necessary?" Does it make you happy? (Yes, I do genuinely use this, and it is effective. Marie Kondo, many thanks!) You'll ask yourself the same questions while at the mall or on Amazon because you'll have thought about it so much that sooner or later, you won't be able to get it out of your head any longer. And most of the time, "NO" will be the response. Voila.

When you stop sorting your belongings and simply donate the ones you no longer need, you will know you are on the right track. Not minimising is organising. Instead of asking yourself, "Do I really need this?," it is simply placing items in bins or baskets or removing them.

The best approach here is typically to dump everything on the (clean) floor and go through the mountain item by item while asking the questions listed above in addition to: "How many of them do I/we truly need?"

I have four towels right now. I do, in fact, have two. The furnished apartment I rent has two. Additionally, I have a washer and a dryer. So I'll have new towels again in two hours. You ask, and what about the guests? That is the issue, though. I have room for eight towels. The truth is that I don't have many guests, so four is fine with me.

Additionally, I only have three sets of sheets per bed (two would be enough). They also arrived with the apartment. However, even if they belonged to me, I would leave them behind when I moved and simply purchase two new sets wherever I went.

When you ask, "How much of this do we actually need?" this is what happens. You can argue that it's false or fight against it, but that won't change the fact that you can get by on a lot less than you might think.

This does not imply that you should have nothing in your apartment or home. Three lovely paintings hang in my living room. And as you suspected, it is. They arrived with the apartment. However, this does not preclude you from having anything. You can possess items. However, they must be items that "spark delight" for you and that you love. Therefore, minimalism does not entail purging one's possessions. It entails getting rid of what is extraneous. As a result, there will be plenty of room for enjoyable, practical, and beautiful things. In this context, "useful" indicates "Do you actually utilise them?" Rather than "do you think you will use them someday in the future?"

To cut a long storey short, you must adopt a minimalist way of thinking in order to become one. And a minimalist will frequently ask themselves, "Do I really need this?" Is this helpful? Whether I adore this The priorities of minimalists are what they need and what they enjoy.

BECOMING A MINIMALIST

Yes! You are reading this book, so I can sense that the minimalist force is already strong within you. So, how exactly does one become a minimalist? The gist is that you should study numerous books about minimalism and then put what you learn into practise. I'm done now. Simple, huh?

That's what I did, at least. I developed my own technique after learning different things from each book; initially, Mari Kondo's book The Magic of Tidying Up had the biggest impact on me.

It also took time to develop. It took place gradually. My cupboard was the first room to be organised, followed by the living room, kitchen, bathroom, and office. I successfully organised my space, but I still had an excessive amount of belongings. The secret minimalist in me began to nag me with questions such, "Why do you need 30 T-shirts if you constantly wear the same ones," after noticing that I consistently wore the same six or seven T-shirts when looking in my cabinet.

I quickly adopted a new strategy and started throwing things away. I began my journey toward minimalism by purging my possessions of anything I didn't need. Later, I'll expand more on how I accomplished that.

However, reading numerous books about minimalism is insufficient. Finding your unique minimalist aesthetic is where the fun begins. What must vanish? What do you opt to save? This is very intimate. Some people (like myself) can live without a toaster or a Nespresso coffee maker, but others can't.

For the longest time prior to beginning my Minimalist journey, despite living alone, I had ten bath towels. Actually, I consistently used these two (because they were fluffier than the rest). After one purge, I had six.

Later, there was another purge. Since Natalia and I don't often have guests over, if I had been really strict, I would have kept only my two favourites. Although it will be challenging to find towels that are as fluffy, we will leave the towels if we move again.

The question of "WHY do you want to become a minimalist" is more significant than "How do you become a minimalist." Because you will discover the HOW once you identify your WHY.

Consequently, WHY do you want to live simply? Consider it, then jot it down here:

HOW TO CREATE A MINIMALISTIC HOME

This was supposed to be a lengthy chapter in which I provided detailed instructions on how to design your minimalist home and what it ought to like. I recently read a chapter about the ideal minimalist home in another book, and it really turned me off. I consider myself a minimalist, so I'm not sure how this chapter would affect you.

Who am I to tell you how YOUR minimalist home should look, I wondered aloud at the same time. I'm not a decorator or interior designer. I have no knowledge whatsoever about that. Regarding colours or how much furniture should be in your minimalist home, I have no notion.

Since I formerly lived on a boat, where decisions essentially made themselves, I am familiar with what a minimalist home looks like. I can also spot a messy house when I see one. Too much things in not enough room. lack of breathing room and fresh air.

I'll leave it to you to decide, then. I have faith that you'll be able to tell when your house is too minimal for you. Your decluttering procedure will result in your minimalistic home.

Okay, so a minimalistic home doesn't include items like stuff stacked on surfaces or large stacks of newspapers, but you already got rid of those while decluttering, right? Your home is another place where "Quality above quantity" is applicable. With the elimination of duplicate items and the maintenance of spotless surfaces, your home already has a minimalist appearance.

What does a minimalist home seem like to you is the most crucial question. And it might well be that if the flat is large, colourful, clutter-free, and feels minimalist to you.

THE DECISION TO BECOME A MINIMALIST

It's amusing. We read a lot of books about how to improve our lives, be happier, and have more time. We attend the conference, do the online course, and speak with a coach. Sometimes nothing changes, and we carry on as before. And occasionally, all that's necessary to bring about a change is to JUST DECIDE TO DO SO. Yup. That's how simple yet challenging it is. I've seen it so frequently.

One of my customers wanted to buy an apartment, meet a committed partner, and switch occupations. Although he is quite attractive and has the funds to purchase an apartment, he hasn't made progress toward these ambitions in the past two years. He had completed his first two objectives five weeks after we began the coaching process. After purchasing an apartment, he met the wonderful woman who would become his wife and the mother of his two children. I wish I could say that everything happened as a result of my fantastic teaching, but I can't. I'm confident it took place because, above all, it was his DECISION that got things moving when he hired me as his coach, spoke aloud about his goals, made a plan, and began working toward them. He was saying out loud for the first time, "I want to buy an apartment. I'm prepared to meet my soul mate. That started the process. It was only a matter of time before he was successful because his decision was supported by a strategy and an action plan.

the same with a different customer. He only managed to increase his success by choosing to improve himself and do so—demonstrating his devotion by working with a coach. He had his finest business month ever in the final month of our collaboration. Once more, I'm confident that 80% of his success was the result of his DECISION to succeed more and to become the finest version of himself. It may resemble woo woo. But certain things in life are illogical and cannot be explained. Sometimes we have to demonstrate to the cosmos, god, and everything else that we are open to receiving.

This is something that I have repeatedly observed taking place. Although I can't guarantee that it will always work, I will guarantee that if you don't even try, it won't.

Decide now to live a basic lifestyle.

LESS IS MORE

Yes, I am aware. That one, I'll bet, has been heard before. And it's true.

Less possessions translate into more time, money, independence, reduced stress, and decreased anxieties.

You'll be well on your way to being a minimalist once you accept the adage "Less is more."

There are several benefits to minimalism. It's the mental clarity it gives me that matters most to me. With less possessions, happiness and living are just made so much easier.

Despite the fact that I'm not very good at cleaning, my house is always tidy. There will be less to dust and clean.

And trust me, cleaning a clear floor and empty worktops is a breeze.

Moving things from one location to another and back is a large part of cleaning for many individuals.

Shopping with a purpose is another major issue. Here is my ruse. I enjoy shopping at outlet malls. That's potentially hazardous territory for a former shopping junkie. Okay, not any longer.

Typically, I arrive there knowing exactly what I need, and I don't shop based on emotions. I don't have any emotional gaps to patch. Additionally, I never make a first-round purchase. Yes, you heard correctly. I therefore browse the entire mall just once while making mental notes of things I find appealing. Maybe I'll even create a list on my phone.

After that, I continue my round. Funny thing is, 90% of the things I liked in the first round I either don't like now or don't require. I always leave the mall without making a purchase. This helps me save money and keeps my cabinets at a minimal level.

I have a lot more money to spend on the things I love, like travel and experiences, as a lovely byproduct of not spending money on things I don't need. I also have no debt, which helps me sleep well at night and have almost no worry most of the time.

Therefore, minimalism encourages thoughtful purchasing while rejecting mindless shopping. You only purchase what you actually need, which is frequently not a lot. I also avoid "sales," etc. Only what I need is purchased. I don't buy products just because they are on sale if I don't need them. So have that in mind. This could also happen gradually, but the better you get at only purchasing what you actually need, the more careful you become when shopping. You'll have more money to pay down your bills, which is a fantastic side effect.

Knowing what you have also entails having less. This is not always the case when you have a lot of possessions. Many of the things you own are likely forgotten. Being able to find items requires knowledge of your possessions. It also involves being aware of what you lack. Keep in mind the six boxes I waited three years to open. Yeah. That won't occur any longer. Knowing what you lack prevents you from wasting time hunting for it. Simply borrow, rent, or purchase it. You'll save a tonne of time and stress by doing this.

More time equates to less stuff. More time for the things you enjoy doing comes from less cleaning, finding, and organising. I explained. This is magic. I'm eagerly awaiting your transition to a minimalist way of life. You'll be telling me in a short while (hopefully), "Marc! You were accurate. I feel liberated in a way I've never felt before because I have so much more time now.

Say "YES" to the idea that less is more and bid your clutter farewell.

BECOME DETACHED FROM MATERIAL BELONGINGS

Life gets much better after you let go of material possessions. It's difficult since, frequently, there are underlying factors that contribute to our consumerism, such as low self-esteem or an emotional void that we could be trying to fill by going shopping for pointless items.

I'm not sure what happened first in my situation. Is minimalism the result of my inner healing and realisation that brands don't really signify anything or was it the opposite? Did adopting minimalism and the decluttering process help me grow and heal? Who cares? Is it even relevant? The outcome is identical. Going to the shopping with me is no longer enjoyable because I hardly ever buy anything, but I'm content and feel much lighter.

To feel whole, I don't need a large vehicle (but sometimes I rent one). I learned that owning a home is not ideal for my way of life. I'd choose to rent. Freedom and independence are two of my fundamental beliefs, so that should explain it.

Spending money on experiences and people makes you much happier, according to my research on happiness (please note that this is NOT a request for financial assistance). I like to spend money on charities rather than items.

I prefer not to be burdened by a property or a mortgage, especially in these exciting times where things change so rapidly. I object to any sociological or political changes. I pack my one bag and purchase a one-way ticket to a nation that either treats me better or is more stable. Although it is unpleasant, it is what it is.

I've learned that having too much stuff simply makes me feel burdened, but like I said at the outset, everyone's definition of minimalism will be completely different. In the end, I hope that this book will—if you choose to—help you improve your life. If not, I hope I at least kept you amused.

THE BENEFITS OF MINIMALISM

Let's discuss the advantages of minimalism. Are your material possessions so many that they are overwhelming? Do you have a hard time finding things? Are you aware that you possess a surplus of items but are unsure of how to dispose of them or what to get rid of first? Have you heard of minimalism and how content people with less stuff are? Do you realise it's time to let go of some of your possessions but are unsure of how to proceed? Or perhaps your clutter is draining you. This book is for you if you can relate to any of the aforementioned issues or simply desire to live a more time-efficient and structured lifestyle.

Want more inspiration? Here are just a few of the innumerable advantages of leading a simple life:

• There will be more time. Fewer possessions mean less time spent arranging and maintaining them and more time for your favourite activities. Additionally, you'll produce more.

• Your finances will improve. You'll undoubtedly spend less since you'll become aware of your spending habits, put an end to impulse purchases, and limit your shopping to items you actually require.

• Your life will be of higher quality. Your life will have advanced as "quality over quantity" becomes your motto as you accumulate superior rather than inferior possessions.

You feel liberated. I've already mentioned how much my possessions used to weigh me down. Now I'm at liberty.

• Stress levels will decrease. We experience stress from a busy environment frequently unconsciously. The less visual tension, the less clutter. Our surroundings frequently reflect our internal states. When we are anxious or unhappy, it directly affects how we maintain our environment, and vice versa. In a spotless, well-organized setting, creativity soars.

• You'll get more self-assurance. You'll feel proud and accomplished when you gaze at your tidy and uncluttered space. You succeeded, and it feels wonderful.

• You'll start to appreciate what you already have more. You'll only keep the things you truly love and value after the decluttering process. "Joy-sparking" individuals

Along the way, you'll develop a stronger sense of gratitude for everything you currently have.

• You'll purge all the unnecessary items so that you're left with only what you really need. The flow of energy will grow.

• You might find out what the purpose of your life really is—spoiler alert: it's not to amass goods.

You'll serve as an example. Spending less after breaking the consumerism cycle actually helps save the environment. In reality, you're working. Everyone these days talks about wanting to change the world and save the environment, but relatively few individuals actually take action. People "rescue the planet" by glueing their hands to the ground, but they then allow Mummy to pick them up in her SUV and return to their congested homes filled with 80% of the goods they don't need.

• Your clarity and attention will increase. Too much things can make you distracted. You can be distracted by visual distractions, yes. You'll be better able to concentrate on the job at hand if there are less distractions. You'll reciprocate. You'll have more money if you start living the minimum way. Most likely, you'll save so much cash that you can donate some of it to charitable organisations. You'll occasionally have a new beginning. Sometimes all it takes to get things moving again when you're stuck and weighed down is a good cleanse and declutter. Start purging whenever you desire a fresh start or a shift in your life. The universe seeks to fill voids

Are you still motivated? So let's go!

MAKE MINIMALISM A GOAL AND FOLLOW THROUGH

Brian Tracy says that "People with clear, written goals accomplish far more in a shorter period of time than people without them can ever imagine." He is correct! Setting a goal will help you to know where you're headed, which is already 80% of the road to success. All that's left is persistence and patience.

For the longest time in my life, I avoided establishing goals (many times, I set the wrong goals and achieved them). Life has changed for the better beyond my wildest dreams since I started making goals. I have accomplished much more in the past seven years than I had in the preceding forty years, including my highest goals. Although it was not easy, it was entirely worthwhile. Even so, I fell short of all my objectives. not even half of them, perhaps. Furthermore, it's still superior to any previous period in my life. It should come as no surprise that the roughly 2 or 3 percent of those who establish objectives typically achieve them.

Why then don't more people make goals? I believe a lot of individuals just don't understand the value of establishing goals, while others are terrified of failing (or even success). The unsettling aspect of having goals is that you can now compare yourself to something. But there's no need to worry; if you take things slowly and are adaptable, you can eventually accomplish things that you never even dared to dream of. The nicest part is that the objective is irrelevant. It has to do with the person you develop while pursuing your objective.

Setting goals will motivate you to act. They act as a kind of GPS system that points the way. If you put your goals in writing, goal setting becomes much more effective. It will assist you in maintaining your attention on the tasks that advance you toward your objective.

Ten-year goals, five-year goals, yearly goals, quarterly goals, monthly goals, daily goals, financial goals, goals for improving one's physical appearance, goals for one's personal development, goals for romance, goals for one's family, goals for one's health, and travel objectives. Your brain is it already spinning? Sincere apologies. You don't have to complete everything all at once, so don't stress. You can begin modestly.

You'll enjoy it once you realise how much creating goals can affect your life. You will reach a stage when the question is not IF but WHEN you achieve your goal with time and experience.

Write down your objectives. That is even more effective. Your regular exposure to your written goals will motivate you to take action and assist you in setting priorities for your tasks.

In order to achieve your goal of "Living a Minimalist Lifestyle," you must delve further and determine what minimalism means to you and what that life will include. Is it getting the least amount of everything? Does it help you declutter your home?

Create the steps that will help you get there after you are clear on your objective and what it will look like. In the next chapter, I describe how I set goals.

Sharing goals with a friend can help some people stay accountable, while it won't help others. Your decision.

Oh. Yes. One other thing: When working toward your objective, recognise your efforts as well as your accomplishments. No self-punishing is permitted! Remember that you have come a long way from where you were a week or a month ago.

Ready? Next chapter, let's set a few more objectives.

GOAL SETTING CONTINUED . . .

We covered objectives and how they affect your life in great detail in the previous chapter. I don't like long chapters, therefore here is another brief and concise chapter in place of one large one. Setting goals will actually look like this. Observe the directions.

1. Outline your objectives. It demonstrates your dedication to your objectives and will motivate you to act. You'll be able to concentrate better on the tasks that will move you closer to your objective. Along with improving your decision-making, concentrating on your destination will help.

2. State your goals clearly, such as "I'm going to boost sales by 5% by December 2023" or "I'm going to run 5 miles four times a week by November 30, 2023."

3. Divide them into manageable chunks and create a list of all the steps you'll need to take to get there. Make a time

estimate for yourself, and don't forget to give each goal and action item a due date.

4. Don't worry if you don't achieve the goal by the precise deadline you set; it's merely a strategy for increasing attention and a sense of urgency. As I've already stated, I've only succeeded in achieving half or fewer of my goals during the past few years. Even so, these have been my best years, and I'm now focusing on the objectives I fell short of in 2016.

5. Keep in mind that you must commit to your goals and that they must be yours, explicit, and expressed favourably.

6. You give yourself rewards for the work you put in toward your goals rather than just for the outcomes. It is completely banned to punish oneself!

7. Setting goals won't make you happier or prevent you from facing natural and unavoidable challenges, struggles, insecurities, or disappointments along the route to accomplishment. However, having meaningful goals will help you get beyond these challenges and motivate you to keep working for your success and happiness.

8. For me, making a to-do list is very helpful (some people might disagree). Put deadlines for each task, your action steps, the amount of time needed to complete the task, and your action steps on the list.

9. Balance your objectives (physical, economic, social, professional, family, and spiritual). People occasionally neglect certain areas of their lives while thriving in others. Strike a balance.

Last but not least, I'll leave you with the exercise in goal-setting that forms the basis of all I've said so far:

I want you to make a list of your life goals for the next ten years (in 5 years, in 1 year, etc.) I want you to put your thoughts down on paper, but I want you to put what YOU WANT, not what YOU THINK IS POSSIBLE. Go big, then! The scope of your creativity is limitless.

1. How do you envision your life to be in ten years? There are no boundaries. Go huge!

2. What must you accomplish in the next five years to move closer to your objective in ten years?

3. What must you accomplish in a year to go one step closer to your five-year goal?

4. What must you accomplish in the next three months to come closer to your one-year objective?

5. What can you do right away to achieve your three-month goal?

6. Make a list of at least three items and ACT ON THEM!

MINIMALISM = MONEY

Let's speak about a really cool benefit of living simply. You'll end up with more money if you make fewer purchases of goods. The majority of individuals believe that increasing your income makes you richer. Typically, the more money you make, the more money you spend (and I'm fully responsible for this). Spending less is the real key to gaining wealth.

You'll eventually just stop caring about trying to "keep up with the Joneses" or, to paraphrase a popular saying frequently credited to Will Rogers or Dave Ramsey: "You'll stop spending money you don't have on things you don't need to impress people you don't like." You'll come to see that material items don't necessarily bring happiness—in fact, it's often just the reverse. Additionally, merely preserving your possessions might be expensive.

You will therefore have money to spend on things that are much more valuable, such as experiences, if you get rid of all of your superfluous stuff and stop spending money on buying new ones.

You could even be able to pay off your debt. For the majority of my life, I had no debt, which was wonderful. Even when I first started my firm, I only borrowed $200,000 at a low interest rate. I've always leased homes and apartments, so I've never felt like I was behind on my mortgage. I think this explains why I sleep so remarkably well.

I won't owe anyone anything when this book is published. I have a $200,000 mortgage and yet struggle every month since I witnessed it happening to my parents. (That's most likely why I've never wanted to purchase a home.)

Another benefit is that as long as I can carry my one bag with me, I'll never feel like I lost everything in these crazy times we live in.

Not to mention, by adopting minimalism, you will benefit the environment, as excessive consumerism is, or at least contributes to, many of the issues facing our globe.

You may improve the future of our world by making the decision to live simply. However, as I indicated in the start, you should be free to choose not to do this and corrupt politicians and psychopath billionaires should not push their opinions on you (who will get richer in the process).

TRACK YOUR INCOME AND EXPENSES

As you've seen, there are many financial advantages to minimalism, but although it's a terrific first step, it won't magically and instantly solve all your financial issues. More is required than that.

I found that keeping track of my income and expenses was quite helpful. Additionally, five years ago, income appeared to be rather low; yet, it now appears to be quite high. You must give any situation a close examination if you wish to modify it. I took that action. I decided to take a closer look at the money because it was draining out so that I would at least know where it goes.

The first step to having a good financial status is keeping track of your income and expenses, which will offer you a precise picture of your situation.

What (and where) are you spending your money on, and what is your net income?

What monthly costs are fixed and what monthly costs are variable

Monthly expenses are, for example:

- Mortgage or Rent
- Groceries
- Fuel
- Insurances
- Savings for retirement
- Gas / electricity / utilities / Water
- Loans
- Cable
- Phone
- Internet
- Cell phone
- Entertainment

- Restaurants
- Transport

You can see your financial condition in this plan, and you should be able to identify trends and areas where you may reduce expenses.

You are now in charge. I still advise against focusing exclusively on the money that is leaving the house since your attention will draw to you more of that.

I experienced two bizarre occurrences when I began keeping track of my earnings and expenses.

1. As soon as I began keeping track of my daily spending, I developed a spending obsession ("Oh no, it's only the 10th! I've already spent $500!"). As a result, the situation I described above began to take place. Since I was focusing so intently on the money leaving, more money was leaving. I made the decision to track daily but just compile my findings at the end of each month. It succeeded.

2. To make matters even weirder, I titled my Excel file "Expenses 2017" and was constantly having trouble. It may be a coincidence, but ever since I renamed the Excel sheet "Income and Expenses" and realised the power of words (and the subconscious mind), my income has

significantly increased and my expenses have significantly decreased. As I previously stated, you attract or see more of what you focus on.

The first step to attracting more wealth and money into your life, according to many financial experts, is regulating and tracking your income and expenses.

It's worth a go, in my opinion!

WHAT'S UNCLUTTERING?

You must get rid of anything you don't use or need. Period. The fun part is that as soon as you start clearing out the clutter, new things (better products, experiences, friends) can move in. This is magic. It looks as though the cosmos is saying, "Oh. Mary is currently taking care of her belongings and getting rid of anything unnecessary. Give her some brand-new, improved, and more practical items.

The key to decluttering is to let go. However, not simply letting go. It also involves letting go of the fear that keeps you clinging to things you no longer need.

Everything is about energy. Your energy is sapped if your home is filled with unnecessary items. Stuck energy is what clutter is, and it builds up.

So what exactly is clutter? Everything you don't utilise is clutter, as I said earlier. Things that are disorganised, items you dislike, and even incomplete projects can be added to this list.

My decluttering and minimalistic quest began with a cupboard clean-out. Take on the entire bedroom after finishing the cupboard. Continue cleaning up your garage, living room, bathroom, and eventually the entirety of your home and office. Get rid of everything you no longer need, including old clothing, books, CDs, furniture, and more. It will be incredible. In the upcoming chapters, I'll go into greater detail about it.

Why have you put off decluttering thus far? Most likely because it is so overwhelming. Prior to succeeding, I also made a number of unsuccessful attempts. When you start decluttering, many unpleasant feelings surface, so we choose to put them off rather than face them. However, that is not a fix. Never is not dealing with feelings.

The most frequent feelings include: • Regret (Why the hell did I buy that? Fear (What if I need this one day?—see above) • I never wear it

Also, guilt. (My mother, uncle Jack, and buddy Tom presented this to me. I am unable to discard this.)

The two hardest feelings to deal with are guilt and fear. Because of this, I think Marie Kondo's strategy is excellent. You start your decluttering process with clothes using her KonMari Method. Afterward, towels, linens, etc. When it comes to making selections regarding what should stay and what should go, you are an expert because you have made hundreds of decisions regarding highly emotive objects like gifts, photos, or cards. By then, making decisions regarding the sensitive issues will be much simpler.

Whenever I declutter, I frequently give things away for nothing. It simply improves my mood, and I intuitively believe that life, god, or the universe will reward me for it.

In a single weekend, one of my clients decluttered his entire flat. He felt so much better and lighter, and he gained energy, which enabled him to complete several of his short-term objectives. He never turned around. The following chapter is his account of events in his own words. It first featured in my book 30 DAYS—Change your habits, change your life as Chapter 31.

One fantastic thing that transpired after I decluttered my physical belongings was that I got on such a roll that I started decluttering the non-physical clutter in my life, such as needless unpleasant emotions, unhealthy relationships, and unreliable business partners. It was amazing. Even now, I am able to pinpoint the precise month that was a key turning point in the beginning of my achievement. 2017 December. I ended three unhealthy business connections that frequently gave me trouble (bad payers and bad clients). Everything suddenly started to shift. I found a technique to sell a lot more books four months later, and the rest is history.

When you declutter, the energy begins to flow once more.

The challenge is to keep your space clutter-free once you've done your first purge and uncluttering. It will start to accumulate again, but if you keep an eye on where, it will be simpler for you.

For me, it's the living room table, kitchen counter, bathroom countertop, and bedroom drawers (which double as my home office desk).

Clutter slowly accumulates. Typically, you are unaware of it until it is too late. I keep these surfaces clean because here is where clutter typically accumulates and attracts more mess. Certain surfaces require daily maintenance. Make it a routine to maintain these surfaces clean, to hang your coat when you enter, and to remove any money or mail from your countertop. Your keys should have a designated spot, and you should use it every time. Every three months or so, I purge my wardrobe as well. merely in case.

Therefore, the KEY question is: When will you begin decluttering?

Action Step: Plan a weekend to purge things you no longer need! PLAN THE WEEKEND RIGHT AWAY!

HOW TO START UNCLUTTERING? GO FOR SMALL WINS!

Once you begin your journey toward simplicity, you attack it like you would anything else. little steps successively till you succeed.

Even if I've heard about folks who accomplished it, you don't have to declutter your entire home in a single weekend. The majority of us mortals, though, would be so intimidated by the effort that we wouldn't even begin. Start small, then. Start out as simply as you can while yet being able to manage it. Your cabinet? Overwhelmed? Start with your underwear or socks or T-shirts, but JUST START!

Next, make another little goal for tomorrow, and then another, and yet another. In the process, you'll make a fantastic ally. MOMENTUM. Success is contagious. Success breeds success. And the little victories you have each day will encourage you and eventually add up to a bigger victory.

More people are becoming more minimalist. You'll feel lighter and more liberated after cleaning out your cabinet, so you'll likely go on to the next task. possibly the restroom.

Start with the simplest decluttering effort you can, acquire confidence, experience the joy, and then move on.

I went in the following order: storage space, a bedroom, a bathroom, a guest room, a kitchen, a living area, and a patio.

Keeping the aforementioned in mind, change as you see fit. I started with the spaces that had the least amount of clutter. And I believe I went after the cupboard two or three times before I had the courage to remove anything that wasn't required.

So let's start the decluttering process. I adhered to Mari Kondo's method, as I previously stated.

She urges that you examine every object, and if it doesn't bring you joy, toss it.

So I piled all of my clothes into a mountain and started the performance. I eventually had two mountains. Clothing to keep and clothing to throw away That meant donated in this instance, but it may equally have meant sold, recycled, or thrown away.

The following chapter will have more.

HOW TO UNCLUTTER

You get ten "how to unclutter" systems if you purchase ten books on minimalism. The majority of them have fancy names or the name of the "Inventor," yet they are all essentially the same things that are only written or expressed somewhat differently.

Since it was the first book I read on decluttering (I didn't realise it would turn me into a Minimalist at the time, I simply wanted to experience the Magic of Tidying Up), the "Marc Reklau Super Duper Approach For Uncluttering Your House" is actually based on Marie Kondo's KonMari method. It has elements of various approaches from Joshua Becker, The Minimalists, Steve Scott and Barrie Davenport, Olivia Telford, and others. I won't spend twenty pages trying to teach you how to clean your house because it's not actually that complicated, doesn't have a silly name, and isn't even rocket science.

But I will share with you what worked for me: To begin with, you must set aside time. I've also prepared an entire book on time management if you want to learn more about how to manage your time.

As I asked you in the last two chapters, have you blocked out a weekend on your calendar?

You then require supplies. Long lists with items like cardboard boxes, permanent markers, etc. will be provided by some persons. The location is not here. I employed garbage bags. I'm done now.

I warned you that with this one, the minimalism force is powerful. (I'll add some recommended reading at the conclusion of the book if you want extensive lists and someone to tell you how to clean your house, but it's really not rocket science.)

Okay. The "Marc Reklau Super Duper Method For Uncluttering Your House" is back.

Start by opening the cabinet. Move from one drawer, one cabinet, and one room to the next. In order to build momentum, you should actually begin with what comes naturally to you. That was the cabinet for me.

start with the attire. All extremely sentimental items, including letters, gifts, and other presents, should be put aside. At first, it's really difficult to get rid of these things. They should be placed last since by that point, you'll be accustomed to making difficult choices.

I won't advise you on how many books you ought to keep. Mari Kondo estimates 15 Three books are the only ones you can keep apart from all the books I wrote if you follow her advice. Ha-ha. I'm joking. Your choice. I discovered a fantastic solution. I got rid of half of my library. Half of stuff is in my better half Natalia's apartment, freeing up space in my suitcase.

It can be really daunting to purge. That's why I began by organising only one drawer in my cabinet. then a second. then a second. I just threw all of my clothing on the ground and began organising it. Keep in mind the crucial words that denoted immediate item disposal:

- "This will be useful one day."
- "Maybe I'll need this one day."

- "This reminds me of good times."

You should donate any clothing you haven't worn in at least one and a half years.

Yes, I genuinely questioned whether it made me happy. and when it didn't, it was let loose.

If you're holding onto clothing that doesn't fit because you want to lose weight so you can wear it again, Abandon them. It hardly ever occurs. Using this rule, I got rid of a lot of clothing. For three years, I had three pairs of unworn pants languishing in my cupboard before I mustered the courage to donate them.

Not everything has to be eliminated in the first round. I went through around three rounds before discarding items that could have been eliminated in round one.

So I went to the linens and towels after the cupboard. Never forget to always clear the area. and placed the entire contents on the ground.

Getting rid of things is part of decluttering. not rearranging anything. not moving objects from one location to another. Things must go.

In fact, I wrote a list. I believe Barrie Davenport and Steve Scott served as inspiration.

- purge clothes closet. (Does it spark joy?)
- Purge linen, towels, bed sheets
- Clean out shower
- Purge bathroom cabinets
- Clean off the kitchen table
- Clear off kitchen counters
- Purge 2 kitchen cabinets
- Organize cleaning supplies
- Clean out fridge
- Purge two more kitchen cabinets
- Clean out freezer
- Purge more kitchen cabinets
- Go through paperwork

- Discard old books (Remove all books from shelves and ask, “Does it spark joy?”)
- Get rid of extra accessories
- Papers, Study materials, Online seminars, Business cards, instruction manuals, Greeting cards, birthday cards, pens that don’t work (Rule of thumb: Discard everything)
- Miscellaneous: CDs, DVDs, Valuables, electric equipment, cables, household supplies, samples, kitchen goods, small change, gifts
- Clean, discard, decide where to put things, and decide what you want to keep.

Other rules:

- Discard first, store later
- Storage: ultimate simplicity
- Don’t scatter storage spaces
- Clutter is caused by failure to return things where they belong
- Put bags into another bag (no more than two)

Clutter is everything you don't use anymore. This includes a wide range of items, such as the outdated stereo you no longer use, exercise equipment you bought but never used, automobile accessories, sporting goods, gardening tools, and so on (indeed, you can definitely throw out or sell 80% of the stuff in your garage).

UNCLUTTERING AND TOLERATIONS GO HAND IN HAND – A REAL LIFE EXAMPLE

This chapter can be found in my book 30 DAYS. It outlines my customer Lawrence's experience, who details what transpired when he began organising his tolerations and clearing up his clutter.

"I felt as though I was establishing a new sense of independence for myself as I went through the process of decluttering my life. Before I knew what cluttering was, I had been going through life acquiring so many negative habits and depressing attitudes. They weren't vice-like behaviours like drinking or smoking, for example. They were more like minor tolerations that seemed inconsequential at first, but as I accepted more and more of them as facts of life that I couldn't change, they grew heavier until I was heavily burdened.

I felt like I was moving like a sloth as a result of these tolerations. Procrastination, lack of sleep, dissatisfaction with my work, a habit of ordering takeout frequently, beating myself up for not being more successful, etc. I must have lost sight of my life's objectives along the way because I simply let these tolerations to clog up my life to the point where I felt stuck.

I had never heard of decluttering until my coach Marc first brought it up to me. I knew what it meant right away, but I had no idea why I was acting this way or how to change it so that I could get out of the hole. I can now identify my tolerations because to the tools Marc helped me acquire, and I'm working on unloading them.

The ones that I could easily solve, such as the window sill that wouldn't open, the paintings I put in storage when I moved, and the uncomfortable old mattress, I swiftly identified and got rid of.

I am always working on the tolerances that will take more time to overcome, such as pushing myself harder at work and enjoying the satisfaction that comes from being productive. To keep track of them all and to hold myself accountable, I've written them down, and I continue to do so when I come across new tolerations.

I feel 10 times lighter now that I have decluttered the tolerations in my life that were jumbled up in my mind and slowing me down. I am more energised, inspired, and enthusiastic. I discovered that as I decluttered the tolerations, so did my immediate physical environment. I feel like I'm living in a clutter-free environment now that my place is cleaner and more spacious."

STAY CLUTTER-FREE

Just wait till you realise how difficult it is to maintain a clutter-free environment. The universe wants to fill all this extra space once more.

So how can you avoid clutter?

- Make sure everything has a home, and put everything back where it belongs.
- Establish a plan. This means group like items together, keep items close to where you'll need them, and organise frequently used items in locations that are simple to access.
- Just as I arranged my cabinet using the KonMari Method, I did the same with my clothing. It looks fantastic. I'm hoping it's not the start of an obsession with something.
- Consider your purchase carefully.

- When something new comes in, the previous one must leave.
- Throw away items and let go of attachment. The more times you go through the process of decluttering, the better you'll get at it.
- Purge clutter frequently because it tends to accumulate slowly and without your knowledge. Check things frequently to see if they are still needed or if they have just accumulated clutter.
- Make sure something old leaves before something new enters your closet every six to twelve months (perhaps even every three to six months).
- Put a stop to things moving inward.
- Keep track of what you truly need, limit the number of times you go shopping, and consider your purchases.
- When you need something that you believe to be absolutely important, wait before purchasing it. If you desire or need it, note it down and wait a few days—sometimes even seven to fourteen—before deciding.

WHEN SOMETHING COMES IN, SOMETHING HAS TO GO OUT

Every time something new enters, something old must leave. You want to maintain the decluttered state of your home after you've done so. And in order to keep it that way, you must follow the aforementioned rule; otherwise, your home will quickly get congested once more.

It's amazing and almost magical. You may give it a shot at home. Make space in your house, garage, or pantry if you want anything new to join your life. The universe seems to be trying to fill all the voids.

In the previous few years (when I still had a lot of stuff), I uncluttered whenever I felt stuck. Something new had undoubtedly entered my life. New opportunities, fresh inspiration, and new acquaintances. Those don't seem to be coincidences. I mean, if it occurs every single freakin' time, how big of a coincidence can it be?

Additionally, I notice it in other people. Let's name her Nadia. She was operating her business reasonably well, but she continually yearned for more, which never materialised. Then all of a sudden, possibly subconsciously, she felt the need to purge. Her home was actually pretty messy. She therefore gave away half of her possessions. A lot of things are simply kept around "in case she needs them one day." Her phone keeps ringing now. I don't take offence if you believe this is hogwash, but I can see why. If I hadn't repeatedly discovered the miracle of decluttering, I would likely believe the same thing.

Did I mention that I only own 18 T-shirts left and often wear the same seven to eight every day? I recently disposed of two items that no longer "sparked delight." Additionally, I own three pairs of jeans. I wear the same pair 80 percent of the time.

Anyways. You must first toss something away if you have a lot of possessions and wish to make room for the universe to fill. You can also go the other way if you don't already have a lot of possessions. There is a new arrival. Consider that when two new pairs of jeans, two T-shirts, and a sweater are added, two pairs of out-of-date clothing must be removed. One pair of shoes must be replaced if I buy new ones. I've just accomplished something that no woman will ever do. Only three pairs of shoes are mine (one pair is in Natalia's apartment). Of course, ladies could accomplish it, but you're not required to. As I suggested in the outset, develop your own minimalist aesthetic.

Of course, this also applies to pots, dishes, and other items. But since I don't own any of those, I constantly think of examples involving clothing. I can still picture the twenty cushions that came with my boat. You guessed right—six were kept.

Stop letting things come in from the outside. If not, your home will quickly become messy once more. Therefore, there should always be less money coming in than leaving.

Make a promise to yourself that you won't ever purchase something again until you are very certain that you will wear or use it. Don't buy something if you think, "I could use it someday." Don't buy it if you believe "This might be handy." Purchase only items you adore. If you must, consider whether you look decent in this. AVOID BUYING IT.

Think twice before you buy. It's not really enjoyable to be at a mall with me, as I've already told you. I am already aware of my needs. I then go through each store once and make a mental list of items I want to buy, but I don't make a purchase the first time. After taking the second round, I realise that I don't need 95% of the items I had originally planned to buy. When I "go shopping" at a mall, I typically leave empty-handed. Boring? Yes! But that's the reason I maintain a minimalist and clutter-free home.

Never go shopping when you're feeling depleted emotionally. It's comparable like going to the grocery store when you're hungry. You frequently purchase items that you don't even enjoy.

Don't buy something right away if you don't absolutely need it. Instead, put it in writing. After a week or two, if you still want to buy it, go ahead and do so.

QUALITY INSTEAD OF QUANTITY

After getting rid of the majority of my unnecessary possessions, I made a promise to myself (inspired by Joshua Becker's book Simplify) to purchase fewer items of higher quality. I decided to buy 10 high-quality T-shirts that I really like instead of 40 (!). There is certainly space for growth because I still catch myself wearing the same five or six T-shirts every day.

This is how I now approach everything. When I have to purchase something, I choose for high-quality products. Because cheap is typically not too durable, cheap is pricey. Low-quality products just don't endure, so if you purchase them, you'll find yourself back in the store a few months later.

I only have around five sweaters and three really good pairs of jeans. You might or might not require additional sweaters if you reside in a cold country. I should probably get some sweaters because where I currently reside in Hungary, the winters may get quite chilly. I understood I didn't require one. Because of the excellent quality of my winter coat, I can stay warm by pairing it with just a T-shirt. How many winter coats do you think I have? Right. Two. Additionally, I have a dryer. You guessed it: it was a part of the apartment. That comes in handy when I need to wash my incredibly warm jacket. I can return to the chilly outdoors in two hours.

Quality over quantity is a principle that applies to many aspects of life. furniture, linens, towels, and even people in the kitchen! I only have a select group of good buddies. Life is ultimately too short to put up with mediocrity.

In every area of your life, favour quality above quantity.

IT'S JUST STUFF

I don't own a lot of things.

Three pairs of shoes and three pairs of flip-flops are available to me. 3 pairs of jeans. (You already know that...)

Aren't you constantly sporting your top five shirts when you take a closer look at what you're wearing? Your six favourite t-shirts, your three favourite sweaters?

After realising that, I got rid of a lot of things.

There is a cost involved when I tell you that all I own fits into a single suitcase. I've purchased three coffee makers, two toasters, two grills, two TVs, two projectors, and two cold press juicers in the last five years, which I eventually gave away. That's all right with me. A tiny amount to pay for mental tranquilly.

I only have three pairs of shoes, why is that? because most of the time I'm just wearing two of them.

Less possessions also means you are familiar with where everything is.

I recall switching from my house to my boat at that time. Six boxes that had not been opened since my prior move were discovered. These cartons had been untouched for six years. I assumed that nothing significant was contained there. I nevertheless opened them and subsequently wasted 90% of what was inside. The contents couldn't have been that significant if I hadn't missed them for six years, and they weren't.

Okay. I'm going to say something even though it could be challenging.

Most of the things you own are only objects. Yup. No matter how crucial you may consider these things to be, they are but things. You won't even miss 90% of this stuff, I promise. You are not required to get rid of it right away because of this. Observe. It's probably simply stuff and can go if you haven't touched it in two or three years.

Less possessions will reduce the amount of worry you have. Keep in mind the proverb, "What you own owns you." The less you own, the less owns you, after all. Additionally, keep in mind that once you leave this place, you won't be able to take anything with you because "the last shirt doesn't have any pockets." Get rid of the excess stuff in your life so that you can spend the remaining time with your loved ones, laugh with friends, go nature walks, or read amazing books rather than stressing about where to put it or who will get your stamp or thimble collection.

Reduce immediately and keep in mind that it's all just stuff.

ELIMINATE EVERYTHING THAT ANNOYS YOU

Your energy is sapped by everything that makes you angry. We refer to this as "tolerations" in coaching. The minor things that deplete your energy may go unnoticed yet are tolerations.

You may focus on 50 to 100 things once you have identified them. Not to worry. It's typical.

For example, a light bulb that has to be changed, a button missing from your favourite shirt, a soiled shower curtain, a dent in your automobile, a cluttered guest room, a drawer stuffed with useless items, broken tools, a cluttered desk, or out-of-style clothing.

All of these are tolerated behaviours that deplete your energy even when you're not aware of it.

Finish your unfinished business since everything left undone is also an offence. This applies to tasks like making phone calls, sending emails, and even finishing up relationships.

Many of your tolerances will go once you start cleaning up. Your life will become more and more clear as a result, and more and more energy will be released.

You're next:

• Make a list of everything that irritates you at home and at work; don't worry if it includes 50–100 items. It's typical.

• After you've listed everything, arrange the items together:

Which ones are manageable? Which are YOU capable of handling? Leave those who don't depend on you for the time being.

I've observed time and time again that if you take care of the issues you can handle, some of the tolerations that are independent of you go away on their own. It's amazing.

Make that list now! Do it right away!

TIE UP LOOSE ENDS

Magic happens when you resolve unresolved problems in your life and complete unfinished business. It appears that it's harder for fresh, better things to enter your life while there remains unfinished business. Even though you occasionally aren't aware of it, a lot of energy is constrained and a lot of space in your thoughts is occupied. You're weighed down by unfinished business.

Bringing order to the decluttering and reducing process also includes tying up loose ends.

Therefore, return anything you've borrowed, pay back any money you owe, show forgiveness to those you've shown it to, and beg for forgiveness when it's due. I know. It's challenging. And it's worthwhile.

Do what you've promised to do. Every commitment you make that you don't keep, every promise you don't keep, drains your energy and affects your mental health. Avoid making commitments you can't maintain. Avoid making promises you can't keep. Make it a rule for yourself never to agree without thinking if someone asks you to commit, attend an event, or perform them a favour if you frequently do so and later come to regret it. buying time "I'll look into it and let you know later," say you. After giving it some thought, you can respond.

Words have great power. The issue is that if you repeatedly violate your promises, not only will people stop believing in you, but you'll also stop believing in yourself because you'll start telling yourself things like, "My word has no value. As a result, I am useless in myself.

Don't let things go this bad. Consider the worth of your word before acting, and do so.

GET RID OF ENERGY ROBBERS

Getting rid of a lot of energy drainers that you probably weren't even aware you had is a great side effect of decluttering.

Your energy plays a key role in propelling you toward your objectives, mental clarity, and enjoyment.

Your existence consists of both things that contribute energy and things that deplete it. Never undervalue the value of energy, and keep going!

When you have low energy, you don't feel good, you're not joyful, and you radiate negative energy. It's likely that you will attract the same kind of energy that you are radiating.

We are all aware of the traditional energy drains, such as poor eating habits, use of drugs or alcohol, caffeine, sugar, or tobacco, lack of exercise, pessimism, sarcasm, or even people. But did you realise that having too much of anything may also sap your vitality? plus a lot!

This is one another justification for the amazing effects of decluttering and living simply. Energy wasters are eliminated. Eliminating distractions, completing unfinished business, letting go of tolerations, and bidding farewell to any connections and people who drain your energy are all part of the uncluttering process.

STOP SPENDING TIME WITH THE WRONG PEOPLE!

One of the major things I didn't expect when I decided to live a minimalist lifestyle was that after purging my home's rooms and cabinets of anything I didn't need or like, I continued to do so.

I started cleaning up my connections. It was a desire. Energy also has a role. Contagious attitudes and emotions exist. People close to you can inspire you, give you courage, and help you take the right decisions, but they can also bring you down, sap your strength, manipulate you, and prevent you from accomplishing your goals in life. Occasionally, spending time with this type of friend could harm your reputation (birds of the same feather . . .).

Be selective about the company you keep. Spend time with individuals who inspire you, who believe in you, and who bring out the best in you. Spend time with people who inspire you. If those around you try to persuade you otherwise, it will be tough for you to develop and flourish.

This also applies to professional connections, and it's astonishing what happened when I decluttered them. When I had completed purging "things," I felt compelled to examine my interpersonal ties. Three commercial connections popped up. They contributed 25% of my revenue, but when I analysed them, they looked terrible. They were really poisonous.

The other two were terrible payers who consistently paid very late. One only called with negative news and difficulties. never running out of justifications for not being able to pay on time. So I made the decision to leave things amicably and thought, "Uh uh, Marc. I'm assuming you'll earn 25% less the next year.

You won't believe what transpired next, or perhaps you foresaw it. I did not have 25% less at the end of the year. I had a 15% increase. In retrospect, it makes sense. I had a lot more room in my head and my life, so instead of chasing after money or resolving the issues of difficult clients, I spent my time being creative, writing more, and increasing my income.

It's no accident that I set the groundwork for my success today just three months after leaving these relationships. It becomes more distinct the more I consider it. If I were to identify the exact moment that my success began, allowing me to live the life of my dreams today, I would mostly point to the moment that I started living a basic lifestyle. This was undoubtedly the turning moment, and if you want to see it from a metaphysical perspective, I proved to the universe, god, and everyone else that "I'm ready" by "getting rid of something that keeps me back." I'm assuming a danger. In the right direction, I'm moving. Send more positive energy my way.

Since then, I've witnessed a lot of individuals experience the same thing. Good things will happen if your relationships are cleaned up.

What would you do if it were family members? The only thing you can work on is improving yourself as a person. Negative people will quickly stop interacting with you if you continue to grow and develop since you are no longer useful to them. If you don't provide them with someone who shares their negativity, they will look elsewhere. If that doesn't work, you really need to consider if you should start to visit them less frequently or stop seeing them altogether. But you have to decide that for yourself.

Make a list of all the people you know and spend time with in your life as a first step (members of your family, friends, colleagues).

2. Consider who lifts you up and who brings you down.

3. Spend more time with the positive individuals and less time, if not none at all, with the toxic individuals (blamers, complainers) in your life.

4. Decide to surround yourself with upbeat, encouraging individuals.

STOP CRITICIZING

De-cluttering your mind is a necessary component of de-cluttering everything. I don't want to delve too deeply into it, but let's look at certain negative habits that are best avoided, and criticising is one of those. It is horrible and completely pointless.

I shouldn't be writing it because I absolutely detest criticism, especially when it is presented as "helpful."

It is outmoded to believe that criticism can make something better. Criticism can demoralise family members, friends, coworkers, and employees and only serves to increase resentment. Because it wounds our pride and puts us on the defensive, it is harmful.

Additionally, those who criticise are typically unsuccessful themselves. Only average individuals have the time to berate their friends. Successful people typically don't have time for quibbling since they are too busy being successful.

Last but not least, research shows that when our positive behaviour is recognised and acknowledged, we learn more, improve faster, and produce more than when we face pressure and punishment.

A critical remark such as "Pete, this is really significant for us," made immediately before a crucial presentation. While encouraging and complimenting a person's skills, such as "John, I like how you prepare these presentations," might put a person up for failure, saying "Don't screw it up like last time" can set the person up for success. Go out there and hit it out of the park" can close the sale.

Don't get me wrong. People who are more successful and have accomplished what I aspire to do can criticise me with open arms. Funny thing is, they never voice criticism! You are only made stronger by them. Only people with little brains criticise because they are either cowards, incapable of producing anything on their own, or both.

Instead than attempting to influence others, try altering yourself. Be the example and the change that you want to see in others.

Critiquing others won't accomplish anything positive. Take the criticism in stride and focus on improving yourself.

STOP GOSSIPING

The harmful habit of gossiping is another pointless behaviour that will only waste your time and possibly even alienate your pals.

Refrain from engaging in gossip and rumours since they are hurtful and destructive. I am aware that it might occasionally be incredibly alluring to hear the most recent rumours from others. I have to be. It serves as the foundation for entire entertainment and TV productions. Following rumours prevents you from working hard and achieving achievement.

I'll say it again since I feel like I say it so often: successful individuals don't waste their time and energy gossiping. They need to focus on more crucial tasks.

Most of the time, the individual spreading these allegations is also probably talking negatively about you behind your back. You undoubtedly live among individuals of this kind; if not, congrats. But typically, this person is present. Whom you simply need to mention a rumour to in order for it to spread like wildfire and for them to keep it a secret and remain silent about it. Bam. It will spread rapidly.

If you are the one spreading the unsavoury rumours, what happens to your reputation is even worse. What if the same logical conclusion I just presented is reached by your listeners? The worst thing that can happen to you is that once they turn them to YOU, they begin to wonder what you are saying about them behind their backs.

The best course of action is to avoid the gossiping cycle. Change the subject or even say, "Sorry, I really don't like talking about people who aren't here," to accomplish this.

Don't ruin your reputation and relationships by spreading rumours. Engage in meaningful dialogue since it is much more empowering and helpful.

Quit chatting. Be a trustworthy person.

STOP COMPARING

Constant comparison to others is the surest path to pain and unhappiness. Social media depresses us because of this.

Yes, I am a victim of it. There is always someone with more or a greater level of achievement. Someone with more wealth, a better vehicle, a stronger six-pack, a larger workspace, a best-selling book, etc. Move on after accepting it. It's utterly pointless to constantly compare yourself to other people. It is illogical. When you judge yourself against others, you'll experience one of two false feelings: superiority or inferiority. You are you. Period.

The same is true of minimalism. Avoid comparing your minimalist lifestyle to that of others. It isn't feasible. You must act in your own best interests. The trip is yours.

The only person you should be in competition with is the person you were yesterday. It may sound like one of those inspirational sayings on social media, and that's because it is one.

Concentrate on you. Think about how you can improve yourself. Put your attention on developing your strengths. When jealousy (this sneaky MF) enters my mind—yes, it even happens to me—I immediately rephrase the envy into admiration and ask myself how I might achieve the same level of achievement as this individual. How do they behave?

Instead of becoming jealous of those who possess things you do not, get inspiration from them.

Perhaps you might take a break from social media for a while if you find it particularly difficult to work on this assignment.

Due to the fact that we watch other people's highlight reels and contrast them with our own "behind the scenes" movie, which is impossible, studies suggest that social media plays a significant role in the development of envy and jealousy.

You may see photos of me working at the beach, drinking coffee on the beach, and travelling to lovely locations if you visit my Facebook page. Don't fall for it, though. Only a snapshot of a half- or full-hour of my day is shown there. I'm confined in my house working for the other ten hours.

I also don't share my mistakes. Maybe I ought to. You have no idea how frequently I was turned down, made fun of, or otherwise mistreated. It is irrelevant. What we do with these experiences is what matters.

Give yourself a break. Don't assess yourself against others.

STOP COMPLAINING

This is one of the first things that needs to go when we continue to discard mental garbage. the undesirable behaviour of whining. Complaining is a completely pointless action that just serves to increase self-pity and reduce your likeability. Who wants to spend time with a complainer, I'm sorry to say. Yes. Exactly. No one. Maybe excluding other complainers. Complainers are in no way appealing. It's a victim mindset, and since you're in control of your own life, that's not who you are.

I would advise you to complain if it helped and had any positive results. Yet it isn't.

Lou Holtz once said, "Never mention your issues to anyone. 20% don't care, and the other 80% are delighted you have them." I personally abide by this maxim.

And I'll admit that occasionally, I whine merely to let off steam. Nobody is flawless. But as I regain my composure and realise what I'm writing in my books, I correct it.

I have to go find it if I don't have the time.

If people don't like my novel, I'll have to start over and make it better.

I don't hold the government, the economy, my parents, instructors, ex-girlfriends, or ex-bosses responsible for my life. I gain knowledge on how to do so, perhaps by reading a book (or 10), for instance.

I have two choices if I'm not satisfied with my weight: grumble and do nothing, or exercise. perhaps a third. Don't do anything, but at least don't whine.

Therefore, stop whining. You are solely responsible for continuing to smoke, consume unhealthy foods, or give up on your aspirations. You are the one who decides to stay in bed longer than necessary and who chooses risk over uncertainty by pressing the snooze button. Don't hold them accountable for not leading happy lives. Your life is yours! With it, you are free to do whatever you choose. You can advance in the path of your dreams the sooner you obtain this.

Retain in mind where to keep your attention! Complaining about your current situation will draw attention to it and "attract" more of what you find objectionable. You need to break free of this vicious cycle and focus on what you desire.

Encourage your positive objectives and determination to succeed by taking a look inside of yourself. Now go and establish the conditions you desire. Start living and making decisions.

Make a list of all your grievances as a first step.

- Examine: What results have your concerns produced?
- In writing: Convert your grievances into demands.

STOP WORRYING

Back then, I used to worry a lot. It was awful. I was always fretting. Worrying about things I couldn't change in the past, things I couldn't control in the future, or things I couldn't control in the economy, in wars, or in politics.

Even hilarious is the fact that the most of the disasters I was worried about either never materialised or were significantly less terrible in reality than in my fantasy.

The day I boarded a jet whose engine blew up in midair ten to fifteen minutes after takeoff is when everything changed. The engine of my jet exploding in flight was one of the few things I had not fretted about that day, as I had on countless other occasions.

In a paradoxical way, this was one of my worst and best experiences ever. I left it with a severe phobia of flying, which grew over the following months. But I also left with a changed outlook on life, feeling more honest, clear, and like myself—and much less of a worrier.

After that, I began to appreciate life much more since I realised how fast it could end. I know . . . A plane can fly with two engines without any issues, according to my engineer acquaintances, and only one out of every hundred aircraft with an exploding engine crashes. The issue is that everyone on that flight believed that our jet would crash.

This quote from the Dalai Lama is one of my favourites when I find myself reverting to my old worrying habits: "If a problem is fixable, if a situation is such that you can do something about it, then there is no reason to worry. Worrying won't help if the issue cannot be resolved. Worrying serves no useful purpose whatsoever. Such strength.

Mark Twain, who once said, "I've had a lot of anxieties in my life, most of which never happened," comes to mind when I think of this.

No matter how much you worry, neither the past nor the future will be altered! Additionally, worrying rarely improves the situation, does it? Instead, it will make you feel bad and make the present moment disappear.

Making a list of your problems is another thing you can do if you have a tendency to worry a lot. Mark off the ones that are connected to your history and cannot be changed. Then you cross out the future-related items that are almost certainly not going to occur. The ones that are beyond your control can then be crossed out.

You are currently left with the ones that you can control. Only 5 to 15 percent of the concerns you had prior to this brief exercise, in my estimation. You want to have eliminated between 85% and 95% of your problems.

Yes. You probably eliminated between 85% and 95% of your problems by identifying them, letting go of the ones you can't change and that are merely using your energy, though I suspect it's closer to 95%.

Try this at home right away:

Taking action:

- List all of your concerns:

Questions:

Which ones have a connection to the past?

- Which ones have a future component?
- Which of them fall outside of your power?
- Which of these issues can you genuinely address?

STOP JUDGING

The destructive habit of judging other people is another one that won't be helpful for you. Once more, it's a habit that does you absolutely no good other than to make you feel better about a life that is probably not what you want.

Have you ever observed that people who are successful and happy in their lives don't judge or care about the lives of others unless they can make a positive difference in those lives? Think about that.

Because we would prefer that everyone be just like us and behave in the ways we like, it can be challenging to resist the temptation to evaluate others. You might as well replace this negative habit with one that is truly healthy for you, like reading or learning more, since it won't happen.

Sometimes when we have a problem with someone, we need to examine ourselves because we can be harming that person without realising it. For this reason, you have individuals instructing you how to live your life in an unstructured manner, people telling you how to handle your finances, overweight people encouraging you to eat healthier, unorganised and stressed out people delivering seminars on time management, and so on.

Look at yourself before criticising others if there are qualities about them that you don't like. Do any of these things about yourself upset you? When you pass judgement on someone, you are actually passing judgement on yourself. The saying "What Juan says about Pedro, speaks more about Juan than it says about Pedro" is a terrific one in Spanish.

It's really difficult to avoid passing judgement on others, as I already indicated. There is always temptation. I try very hard not to condemn individuals because I have frequently been in the same situations as those for which I have previously judged others. That may be extremely frightening, but it greatly aids in overcoming that destructive habit. I have experienced situations where I was in the same boat as the folks I had previously criticised.

The adage "Walk a mile in my shoes before you judge me" is indeed true to some extent.

Ever since, anytime I feel the want to pass judgement on someone, I think, "Uh, uh. Danger. It's possible that you'll experience the same thing. Do not judge. Do something constructive now.

Before passing judgement on others, practise kindness and organise your own life. Instead of focusing on other people's weaknesses, work on your own shortcomings and, most importantly, your strengths.

ADOPT A POSITIVE MINDSET

Whether you realise it or not, your attitude greatly affects the consequences in your life. Certain occurrences may knock some individuals down or even break them, but for others, it serves as motivation to try again with even more fervour.

The ideas that "there's something good in every awful" or "you just have to find the good" have helped me get through life's ups and downs and may have even saved my life.

How do you perceive the situation? As long-lasting ("Never") or fleeting ("one step closer")? For whom is failure? A failure of a chance for achievement? Which do you prefer, optimism or pessimism? Did you know that, in terms of science, there is only one distinction between an optimist and a pessimist? The way you interpret events is that thing.

Both optimism and pessimism are not inborn traits. It's not a genetic issue. It is possible to develop an optimistic outlook, and doing so increases success. Your biological and psychological immune systems are strengthened by optimism. Finally, but certainly not least, optimists live longer. (PS: There are other factors to take into account, thus this does not imply that all pessimists pass away young. Additionally, it doesn't imply that all optimists have long lives. Being optimistic may not make much of a difference if you smoke 40 cigarettes per day.)

However, not everything in Optimismland is bright and cheery. We must exercise caution over a crucial issue. phoney optimism False optimism eventually results in disappointment, rage, and misery. We must have the skills to be "realistic optimists." Positive thought is insufficient on its own. The recipe for success also calls for optimism, enthusiasm, and labour of love.

Another myth is that having too many expectations can make you disappointed. That is incorrect. As a result, people stop having high expectations for themselves.

Disappointment is more often the result of unrealistic expectations.

The misconception is that we can experience happiness or sadness as a result of events. Mistake again.

Science has discovered that there are peaks and valleys surrounding a fundamental degree of wellbeing. Life will inevitably have its ups and downs, but how you respond to them is entirely up to you.

You have more freedom to take risks, which is wonderful news. Your baseline level of happiness will rise, and that's what it's all about, if you deal with problems instead of trying to escape them, face them head-on, take risks, deal with them, and try new things.

Embrace optimism. Fun is had. (Also, read the works on the subject by Martin Seligman.)

BE GRATEFUL

Are you content with what you currently have or are you constantly on the lookout for something new and exciting? I strongly advise you to start practising thankfulness, no matter where you are in your journey toward minimalism or even if you have no interest in doing so.

The brain is shown to be rewired to focus more on the good things around you after three to four weeks of practising gratitude. You'll become happier, more upbeat, and more outgoing as a result. You'll get more rest and experience fewer headaches. Both your energy and emotional intelligence will increase. You'll learn to forgive more easily and develop a lower propensity for despair and worry.

Daily emails from my readers describe how being grateful has improved their lives. It's simply incredible. One reader shared a home with friends and is now dating the love of his life after leaving his single status and returning to live with his parents. One of my old clients transitioned from a deal where she only received a percentage of sales to one where she got a fixed pay and a fixed contract. When people who are going through a very difficult time in their lives seek me for guidance, I first explain that I can't give them any counsel since I don't even know what I would do in their shoes. Then, because I know it helps, I advise them to practise appreciation.

My miracle cure is gratitude. It serves as the antidote to all the unpleasant feelings that occasionally visit us, such as grief, envy, despair, wrath, and so forth. Gratitude prevents you from experiencing any of those other feelings. I've found that being grateful has multiplied my success. I found that I was happier and had more success the more appreciative I was. Every time I did (even the best of us forget to be grateful. Since we are all human, my results began to decline.

I thus hope you choose gratitude even if you decide not to become a minimalist after reading this book.

It's quite simple.

Every day, either in the morning or the evening, or both, list three things for which you are grateful. Feel the appreciation. I'm done now. It works and doesn't take more than five minutes.

Try it.

(I wrote a book on appreciation if you want to read it in its entirety. One of my favourites is titled The Life-changing Power of Gratitude.)

FORGIVE YOURSELF

The best part is: You don't have to be perfect since you will never be perfect! Simply take minimalism one day at a time and one step at a time. I didn't suddenly start living simply in a month. I cleaned out my cupboard, as I had previously said. I enjoyed it. I went through it again, making sure I hadn't missed anything. Then, after noticing that having less stuff made me feel lighter and better than I had for a long time before to beginning to accumulate stuff, I got rid of even more things.

Like many other things, minimalism is not an easy path to follow. Like so many other things in life, such as success and habits, there will be setbacks, blunders, difficulties, and failures. The most essential thing is to be kind to yourself and to keep trying. When things in life don't go as planned, don't be hard on yourself. Talk to yourself as you would a friend in a similar circumstance, then resume your fight.

Your life will improve with minimalism, and there are many wonderful advantages. In a world that seems to be becoming crazier by the day, a simple existence can help you stay sane. You'll hopefully experience the same emotions that having everything you need—but not everything—gives me: peace, clarity, and freedom. You can do this.

KEEP A JOURNAL

One of the wisest things you can do, minimalist or not, is to keep a journal. I wouldn't trade it for anything; it's one of those things. Amazing scientific research about the different benefits of journaling have just come to light. It enhances focus, reduces stress, and offers a host of other health advantages.

The Department of Psychological Medicine at the University of Auckland in New Zealand discovered in 2013 that journaling encourages quicker wound healing! Compared to the non-journaling group, the members of the journaling group recovered 75% more quickly.

According to other study, journaling lowers absenteeism from work, speeds up the process of finding a new job after losing one, and raises student GPAs. Consider this.

Even fifteen minutes a day of journaling helped people recover from injuries more quickly, boost their immune systems, and raise their GPAs. If there were a medication for it, it would sell out immediately!

Spend a few moments at the end of the day thinking. How did you perform well? What could you have improved upon? What brought you joy today? What can you be thankful for right now? Keeping a journal is a great way to gain perspective. Sometimes you might believe you had a bad day, but when you look back on it, all that happened was John told you something you didn't like at nine in the morning, and the rest of the day was fantastic.

You'll experience greater happiness, motivation, self-worth, and understanding as a result of journaling. It has the wonderful side effect of getting your thoughts focused on something nice right before bed, which is good for your sleep and subconscious mind. Instead of concentrating on the things that didn't go as planned and would likely keep you up at night, you choose to be grateful for the good things that happened today.

Try to respond to the following inquiries each night before bed and record your thoughts in your journal:

- What am I appreciative of? What three things have made me happy today? (Write 3 – 5 points)
- In what three areas did I excel today?
- In what ways could I have improved today?
- What's my main objective for tomorrow?

As you begin this practise, don't worry if the words don't come easily at first. Your journaling will grow better with practise, just like everything else. Simply wait an additional five minutes if you are stuck or unable to think of anything. Don't hesitate to write anything comes to mind, and don't be critical of it. Don't be concerned about your blunders or style. You keep a journal here. Nothing else will be visible. Just write! Do this each day for a month, and then watch the changes happen! Any ordinary journal or calendar will do.

LET GO OF THE PAST

Spending time in the past steals time from the present and the future. Don't hold on to your drama; stop replaying it. SET IT AWAY! You can only be receptive to new things entering your life if you have the strength to let go of the old.

The inability to let go of the past is another indicator of having too much clutter. But as I've already said, if there's too much of the old, new things can't enter our lives. By beginning to organise your space, you may begin to address your issues and make way for new things to enter your life.

On a mental level, letting go of the past is spending less time worrying about things that might have happened, should have happened, or that didn't turn out the way you had hoped. Physically, it entails letting go of things from the past that are no longer useful.

It is not logical.

Get rid of clutter while taking lessons from your past mistakes. That is all you need to do moving forward. Yes, it is simple. Make place for fresh ideas, fresh actions, fresh goods, and fresh connections.

To be free and allow new things into your life, you must let go of the old. Get closure with individuals, conclude unfinished business, and let go of old baggage. So that you can fully appreciate the present, finish the past.

Adopt the mentality that you will always finish your business going forward. In terms of your relationships, your job, and all other areas, don't leave anything unfinished. Continue forward motion.

Taking Action:

What in your life is lacking? Create a list, then work through it!

REWARD YOURSELF

The idea of rewarding yourself as you complete tasks is a crucial topic that isn't discussed enough.

Your concentration and productivity will improve, and you'll feel more inspired to get things done. This applies to everything, not just setting up a simple environment.

For instance, if I write from 7 to 10 in the morning, I normally give myself a two-hour break to check my personal Facebook page and/or watch an episode of my preferred television show. Only if I finish my task and write enough words each day will I be eligible for this reward (2000 words).

Other pleasures I offer myself include going out with friends, taking a power nap, watching a movie or TV show, taking a relaxing bubble bath, visiting one of Budapest's famous thermal spas, or visiting a coffee shop that is more than 100 years old.

You can treat yourself after finishing a task, cleaning a room, or effectively purging a cupboard in the context of decluttering and minimalism. You'll think of incentives. You'll, I'm certain.

Life and work will be much more enjoyable if you develop the practise of rewarding yourself for a job well done.

START

Half of the book has already been read by you. What have you already put into practise?

The crucial phase is getting started. It's also the part that's the hardest. No matter what they do, a lot of people get stuck in the planning or preparation stage. It occurs all over. Salespeople arrange their calls for weeks in advance but never pick up the phone. those writers who have their entire book planned out yet never start or finish their manuscript. The planning procedure has that risk. Even though we frequently put off doing what needs to be done, it gives the impression that we are making progress toward our goals. The most crucial step is getting started.

Just Do It is the greatest approach to get started. You now understand why I enjoy Nike t-shirts. They serve as a constant reminder to do something.

The greatest way to get started is to take one modest step at a time. Maybe clean up one little drawer. You'll have the drive and motivation to proceed to the subsequent work as a result.

I've already shown you how I got started with the decluttering in this book. Yes. I only opened the first drawer. T-shirts I own. I believe I spent two days with the cabinet. Getting rid of more useless items each day.

Everything's not necessary to finish it all at once. Things are hard to get rid of. I tried several times. And as things became better and better, my house and later the cabinet became increasingly empty. You've already figured out that performing little things regularly every day can have a big impact.

So, after all of your preparation and discussion on minimalism, action is required. There won't be any outcomes if nothing is done.

So please, get started right away! with a minor item. What exactly will it be? then proceed to consistently act.

Simply begin with what you have, and take each step as it comes. Take the initial step in faith, as Martin Luther King Jr. advised. You only need to take the first step; you don't need to see the entire staircase.

Taking Action:

RIGHT NOW, start organising one drawer!

100% RESPONSIBILITY

The first step in any transformation is accepting full responsibility for your life. That implies that no one else is accountable for your life. YOU. Not the economy, not the weather, not your boss, not your partner, not your parents, not your friends, not your clients. YOU! I am aware that is frightening. Furthermore, it liberates.

Don't misunderstand me, please. This does not imply that everything that occurs to you is your fault. Sometimes excellent people experience horrible things. However, it is up to you how you respond to these situations.

Everything changes once you stop putting the blame for your life's events on other people.

You change from being a victim of your circumstances to creating them. You assert the right to choose your course of action in response to the challenges life throws at you. You transform from the exterior to the inside (the others must adapt for my benefit) (I decide how something affects me with my attitude).

Change what you can, accept what you can't, and make the most of what you have. The biggest gift of all is that your life is yours. The aspects of your life that you would like to improve are within your power. You have the power. The worst case scenario is that you will no longer have anyone to hold accountable.

You have the freedom to alter your actions, yet life does happen. Almost all of your endeavours depend on you for success. Never overlook the importance of finding solutions. Where you can, take action, and when you can't, accept it. Also, yes. Living is unfair. Adjust to it. When you are aware of your control, things are simpler to handle.

Therefore, it bears repeating: Even if you have no control over the stimuli that the world sends, you have the freedom to decide how you will react to it.

Be the hero of your own storey. Make excellent choices and hold yourself responsible. Live in the present while taking lessons from history.

That is what it is to take full responsibility. You have the power. Nobody is at fault. Nobody will come to your aid. You'll be alright.

Here are some queries that may be useful to you: • Who are you now blaming for your current life situation? (Your spouse? Your manager? your parents Your companions?)

• What would happen if you stopped blaming other people for your life's circumstances?

• How can being a victim of your circumstances assist you?

• What would occur if you decided to transform your life RIGHT NOW?

What changes would you make? Where might you begin? Where would you begin?

CHOICES AND DECISIONS

Every event in life has a purpose, and occasionally that purpose is that you make really poor decisions. This is a joke that I came across on social media, but it contains a lot of truth. Your decisions and choices have an impact on your life. It's excellent that you feel offended by this statement since it means that you can still improve.

Even while horrible things do occasionally happen to decent people, you still get to select and ultimately decide how these things will impact you. Yes. You are actually that strong!

Your current existence is a direct outcome of the decisions you've made in the past, and each decision has an effect. You will achieve better outcomes if you start making smarter decisions. And if terrible things do occur, act like Viktor Frankl.

Jewish psychologist Victor Frankl was detained in Germany's detention camps during World War II. Except for his sister, he lost every member of his family. Even the Nazi jail guards were unable to take away his "ultimate human freedom" as a result of these terrible circumstances because, while they could control his exterior surroundings, in the end, he was the one who chose how they would effect him. While he was powerless to change the situation, he and YOU both had the power to decide how to react. Your life will be significantly impacted by this.

So, remember that there is hope, no matter what you are going through right now. You can get through it. Possibly with assistance from someone (a therapist or coach). Nobody said you had to face this challenge by yourself.

How does this relate to minimalism? I'm not sure. However, making better decisions will improve your quality of life.

Oh. Yes, I just realised it. Decluttering and minimalism are great ways to develop your decision-making abilities. If you use Marie Kondo's organising technique, you'll begin by asking yourself, "Does this T-shirt ignite joy?" "Are 30 pairs of socks really necessary?" Hundreds or perhaps thousands of decisions will be made by you, and what happens if you repeat anything a thousand times? Right! It gets easier as you get better at it.

When the process is complete, you reach the stage where you must make decisions about deeply emotional items and ask yourself, "Does it stay or does it go?" Though making a decision on this is much more difficult, you'll be an expert by that point.

You may then start to decide who needs to leave your life after experiencing something similar to what I did. or with whom you conduct business. whether or whether you purchase a specific course. It really is magical. I become quite skilled at making decisions as a result of minimalism and decluttering.

I bet you never imagined it all began with a simple inquiry: "Does this sock ignite joy?"

SELF-DISCIPLINE AND COMMITMENT

Any new endeavour requires some commitment and self-discipline. Without those two qualities, it will either fail or take a lot longer than it should. Your determination and commitment are crucial components in your path to success. These personality factors will determine if you follow through on what you claimed you would do. Self-discipline entails carrying out your obligations even when you're not feeling it.

They claim that self-control can be trained, much like a muscle, and that the more you do it, the better you get. In fact, I was certain that this was true for a very long period. Well, when it comes to self-control, I'm not so sure anymore. Is it actually self-discipline, or is what it appears to be made up of merely the proper routines and habits?

Consider the past athletes. They must be quite disciplined since some of them gain a lot of weight after retirement. So, did they lose their self-control or did they simply cease practising wholesome routines and habits?

So if you lack much self-discipline, try developing some habits. For habits, you require much less discipline. Just at first, after some time the behaviour turns into automatic and you just do it. similar to how you would clean your teeth.

Do you require determination and self-control to wash your teeth? No? That's because it's a habit, I suppose. Train yourself to be disciplined, develop healthy habits, or do both.

You do, however, need to be committed. Without commitment, success is impossible since it motivates you to keep going. The key to success is no longer so obscure. Commitment and tenacity are necessary. Will you remain steadfast in the face of difficulty? The query is that.

And starting is the best approach to succeed in anything you do. Therefore, quit questioning your level of self-discipline. possibly the habits. simply start working. Additionally, tomorrow. and the following day. Easy. Is it not?

RAISE YOUR STANDARDS AND PROTECT YOUR BOUNDARIES

By how you treat yourself and what you let others do, you show other people how to treat you. Maintain high standards and safeguard your boundaries.

Demand higher standards for both yourself and those around you. This may appear to have nothing to do with decluttering or minimalism at first glance, but it actually does—and a lot!

You must elevate your standards if you truly want to change for the better in your life. Set high standards for yourself and people around you, which is equally important or perhaps more so. Make the decision to refuse mediocrity, procrastination, and conduct that gets in the way of your finest efforts. Make the decision to always be truthful, on time, and to truly listen to others until they are through. Do the little things properly because how you handle them will determine how you handle the larger things.

People can't do certain things to you when there are boundaries. Show those around you what you tolerate and don't tolerate in relationships. Establish clear limits and make it a practise to deal with any issues right away. What are the limits? Here are some examples: People can't yell at you, can't make foolish jokes around you, can't treat you disrespectfully, and you can't either, remembering what I said earlier. Set an example for others to follow.

Maintain your limits and don't give in. If you give in, you're telling individuals you approve of their actions. For instance, if you accept a business call on a Friday at 10 p.m., you're telling the caller that it's acceptable to do so.

Call out anyone who crosses your bounds without delay. Let them know: "I didn't like. . If they continue, tell them to stop by saying, "I ask you to stop. . . The majority of individuals should have understood it by this point, but occasionally one or two persist. If it occurs, insist, saying, "I insist that you. . . "Leave if any of the three steps don't work. I can't have this talk while you are ______, so I'm going to go. We'll speak afterwards.

Your surroundings will show how strong your standards and boundaries are. Test it out. Set boundaries and raise your standards.

Actions to Take:

the following information in writing:

- Aspects of life that you will no longer accept.
- All the conduct that you won't put up with anymore from others.
- Everything you aspire to become.

SIMPLIFY

Condense everything. Period. Liberation, joy, and equilibrium are brought through simplifying. Once you become used to living in a straightforward, minimalist environment, you won't want to leave. On the other hand, you'll frequently yourself yourself asking, "What else can I simplify? Where else can I put aside distractions and just concentrate on what matters most? "

Your life should already be a little bit simpler if you started putting some of the things you have learned so far in this book into practise. Have you decluttered? Organize your cabinet? eliminate a few tolerations? Did you get rid of some of the negative influences in your life? What are your top priorities? Did you schedule time for the things that are truly important in your life?

Downsizing your life and learning to get by with less are key components of minimalism.

When you pay attention to the vital things, life becomes much easier. the crucial. activities that are appropriate for you. Simply get rid of or scale back everything else. Automation, delegation, elimination, or recruiting help are all options for achieving this.

• Is your calendar too full? Eliminate it.

Do you have too many responsibilities? Reject new ones or cancel existing ones.

• Can online banking help you organise your finances?

• Switch to paying with cash and limit your purchases to those you truly require?

• Spend more time with your friends and family in person rather than on social media.

• To avoid being constantly distracted, only check your emails at specific times during the day, and disable the tone of email and SMS delivery.

• Ask yourself if you really need to read three different newspapers every day, and unsubscribe from journals that are just building up and that you never read.

• Do you travel to work? Asking your supervisor to work from home once or twice a week might be possible.

Questions:

1. Where in your life do you see excess?

2. Do you own too many items that you don't use or need?

3. Are you constantly booked?

4. Do you have time in your schedule to be with yourself and engage in the activities you enjoy?

5. What are the most crucial responsibilities in your daily life—at home and at work?

6. Which duties are simple to automate, delegate, or eliminate?

START TO GET ORGANIZED!

Getting organised is just one aspect of minimalism, as I have stated. It involves getting rid of surplus items. But becoming organised can be a good first step, particularly if you're nervous.

You can simply toss away all the papers you have in your home, according to Marie Kondo. For me, that's even too audacious. I mean, important things can happen. Taxes and similar fees. I also decided to sort through all the documents before discarding them. The good news is right here. I discovered after organising the papers that I could discard at least half of them without losing any sleep.

So it could be a good idea to look into this a little if you are surrounded by mountains of paper and have Post-it notes all over your office table.

According to research, executives nowadays spend between 30 and 50 percent of their time looking for documentation. Are you sure about that?

So go ahead and begin sorting and filing your papers, after which you can discard any that are superfluous.

Set your desk aside. You'll be more productive as a result.

Without even thinking about it, journals and newspapers should be discarded, as should papers from classes you took five years ago that you preserved but never again opened.

The impacts of digital clutter are the same as those of physical clutter, did you know that? Although it can be a fantastic productivity tool, your computer can also be the biggest distraction in your life. Your decision.

Marc, one of my customers, decluttered virtually, and it had the same impact on him as decluttering physically. He gained a lot more energy as a result of having a heavy burden off his shoulders.

He took control of his emails as his first action. Emails are a major time waster. Actually, you should complete your most critical tasks every morning before checking your emails, so avoid doing this first thing in the morning (except if your job relies on it, of course). You will become much more productive as a result.

Establish regular hours for reading your emails and using social media. Turn off all notifications, including email and text delivery, and check your emails only at specific times during the day, such as at 9:00, 13:30, and 18:00, to avoid being distracted.

Marc regained control of his email and cleared his computer's desktop. He organised information into folders on his desktop. All unnecessary programmes and apps were uninstalled by him.

He made a folder in his email inbox and put all the emails older than six months into it before using it as a to-do list. Emails that had been replied to were stored in their respective folders, while unanswered emails were left in the inbox. He started to empty his email inbox every day after that.

He never turned around.

HARNESS THE POWER OF THE MORNING HOURS

Despite the fact that this is not a book about time management, you were able to find a few little time-saving tips in it. And I just can't help but incorporate the routines that have been most beneficial to me. You're not the only one who feels as though there should be more hours in the day. I believe that is how most people feel.

A morning routine was one of the major game changers in my life, along with appreciation, minimalism, and the 80/20 rule. WOW. Incredible. Even though I occasionally indulge in laziness, if I have a deadline to meet or need to complete a lot of work, I return to my morning routine. Your productivity and well-being will soar if you establish a morning habit.

The thirty minutes just after you wake up and the thirty minutes right before you go to sleep make up the most crucial hour of your day. Because of how responsive your subconscious is at this moment, what you do is really important.

The course of your day will be significantly influenced by how you begin it. You've probably experienced days that went off to a bad start and then grew better and better, or the contrary, where you woke up with the impression that everything would go your way, and then it did. It's crucial to start your day off right for this reason. Most of us just wake up and start rushing around, and that's how our days go. It's understandable why today's population is so stressed out. What would it change for you if you woke up an hour or more earlier each morning?

This was one of the key characteristics successful people shared, according to my research on successful people. a morning regimen of some kind. I reasoned that there must be something to it if all these successful people have some sort of morning routine. I had better try. When I tried it, it really changed me.

Routines may seem monotonous and inflexible to some people, but for me, they have always led to productivity, freedom, and enjoyment.

When I have to deliver, I get up around 5 or 5:30 in the morning. I took a 30-minute walk to relax. Practice gratitude, engage in some meditation, or just spend some quiet time considering what's most crucial for today (already figured out the day before, before going to sleep).

Because there are ZERO interruptions and distractions in the morning hours between 6 and 9 a.m., I've discovered that I can accomplish twice as much work as I did previously. Additionally, I get a feeling of pleasure and success when I watch other people leaving for work at 9 a.m. while I'm virtually finished for the day. My self-confidence soars as a result since following a plan or routine and succeeding in it gives me a positive feeling.

You feel much more in control and presumably experience less stress when you follow a regular schedule. In your life, you're developing structure and positive routines. Gaining time in your day is all about setting priorities, which this will assist you in doing. Having a morning routine also has some amazing "side benefits," such as the elimination of procrastination and the development of momentum. Not to mention the crucial 30-45 minutes or an hour of "me-time" you gain from rising early.

By including a nighttime ritual, you can improve the outcomes of your morning ritual. The final thirty minutes of your day are equally significant. Your subconscious will continue to process the items you did in the 30 minutes prior to bedtime. If not:

- Consider keeping a journal.
- Consider your day. (What did you achieve well? What else could you have improved upon?
- Make a plan for the day. (What tasks are you most anxious to complete tomorrow?)
- Create a to-do list for tomorrow.
- Imagine the perfect day.
- Read some motivational books, articles, or blog posts.
- Take inspiration from inspiring music.

Before you go to bed, I strongly advise not watching the news or any upsetting movies. This is so that you can make suggestions to yourself as you go off to sleep.

Because of this, it is much more advantageous to listen to or see positive content.

You can benefit greatly and save a significant amount of time by organising your day's tasks in advance. If you are aware of your priorities, the tasks at hand will be ingrained in your subconscious, and you will start working with extreme concentration the following day.

Will you attempt it? I heartily endorse it!

USE THE MAGIC OF VISUALIZATION

Visualization has great power. There is scientific evidence to support the claim that your subconscious brain cannot tell the difference between a skillfully executed image and reality. When a subject was staring at its hand and shortly after, when it visualised its hand, scientists scanned the person's brain. And the results of their brain scan were astounding. The brain regions that were "shooting" in both instances were the same.

Your subconscious mind will be persuaded that your minimalism goals are actually becoming a reality if you imagine them in great detail and with a lot of emotion. Then it will give you the inspiration, chances, and ideas to assist you in changing your life into that desired state.

You can find additional evidence that visualising is effective if you read the interviews of athletes. Several people, including Jack Nicklaus, Wayne Gretzky, and Greg Louganis, are noted for using visualisation to succeed in their endeavours.

You should picture yourself in your visualisation already living in an uncluttered home or apartment and having achieved your minimalism goal. Put all of your senses to work by experiencing it with your own eyes and by smelling, hearing, feeling, and tasting it. It will have a greater effect the more emotion you put into it. Over time, if you do this for 15 minutes a day, you will have great success. Schedule time each day for your daily visualisation, either as part of your morning routine or right before bed.

Making a collage of pictures that symbolise your aspirations and sticking it up in your room or another visible location can be useful. Purchase some journals, and then cut out the images of your objectives. On your desktop or computer, you may also make a screensaver out of a variety of images. Put a picture of your ideal home, some cash, or whatever money means to you if you want to become wealthy. You'll undoubtedly come across a tonne of instances if you Google "vision board" examples.

Every day, five minutes after waking up and five minutes before going to bed, look at your collage and mentally picture yourself having achieved your goal.

complete disclosure Despite my poor imagination skills, I am already living the life of my dreams. It exceeds my expectations in every way. Three years ago, I couldn't have imagined selling 100,000 books annually, relocating to one of Europe's most stunning and vibrant capital cities after living in a Penthouse for an additional 1.5 years on a gorgeous island in the Mediterranean (Budapest, Hungary). I consistently worked toward my daily objectives, practised thankfulness, and engaged in other positive behaviours, and then everything "came into place."

What I'm trying to say is that even if you don't visualise well, if you have a general notion of where you want to go, have formed some positive coping mechanisms, have set objectives for yourself, and are willing to work hard enough, you will succeed. My personal belief has always been that if you try your hardest every day and make tiny, steady progress, a year from now, you will undoubtedly be doing well. Think about in five years.

Taking action:

What kind of setting would you prefer? Make use of every sense. Do you see anything? Hear? Smell? Touch? Taste? Make notes on concepts and specifics, then visit the location daily in your mind's eye.

THE POWER OF SMALL HABITS—CELEBRATE YOUR WINS!

This chapter is intended to lift your spirits a little since we must never lose sight of how far we've already come. Because there is never a shortage of things to be unhappy about (especially for the perfectionists among us), we must teach our minds to focus on how well we have done thus far. We must develop the ability to monitor our development.

So please do me a favour and take a moment now and then to reflect on your progress. Enjoy the fact that you have improved from last week and from a year ago. Many congratulations!

Never ever fail to acknowledge your minor accomplishments. Every step taken in the right direction and every little victory are worth celebrating.

Gratify yourself. Go to the movies, purchase something you've always wanted (after giving it some thought and recognising how much you need it), or do anything else that makes you feel good and joyful.

I typically treat myself to quick excursions or a day at one of Budapest's magnificent spas. I have a cup of coffee in one of the many five-star hotels to commemorate simpler victories. Be original! Will you go to the spa or go out to a great dinner? Will you take a stroll?

Here are some incentives to note:

DO IT NOW!

The best strategy for success is to ACT NOW. Don't wait for certain circumstances or "a sign" to begin. Take ONE STEP IN THE RIGHT DIRECTION RIGHT NOW to get started. I don't have a foolproof recipe for success, but I do have one for failure: putting things off till later, sometimes known as procrastination.

You're definitely putting off organising your cabinet if you've wanted to live a minimalist lifestyle for a very long time. Procrastination can take many forms, like reading more books about minimalism. Stop putting things off; you owe it to yourself greatly.

It really is a pain. It makes you feel anxious and unwell the most of the time. You'll discover that the tasks you put off can be completed in an hour. While some of my friends utilise procrastination to see problems magically improve over time, this is more of an exception than the rule, and I wouldn't advise it. Things typically don't get better on their own and frequently grow worse.

When you put off doing something, you are procrastinating. It's putting things off in the hopes that they will somehow improve while doing nothing to address them. However, procrastination can also take the shape of doing something that is more important than what you should be doing or something that doesn't need to be done (instead of what you should be doing). The latter, though, probably won't cause as much damage.

Procrastination can take many different forms, including being distracted, delaying chores, waiting until a task is perfect before finishing it, and leaving things to the very last minute.

Procrastination is frequently brought on by some sort of worry. Dread of success as well as fear of success itself, rejection, failure, and being evaluated. Another factor is feeling overburdened.

It's incredible how many individuals put off doing things by keeping themselves occupied. Instead of making sales calls, they are creating Excel sheets. They create a grand plan as opposed to merely getting started. Instead of preparing for my examinations, I was constantly cleaning my room.

Procrastination has a significant cost for you. When you feel the want to put off a task—in our case, perhaps decluttering—ask yourself, "What would I lose by putting this off? Is it worth losing sleep and being plagued by a task that I might have completed in one or two hours?

Don't disregard this. Avoid procrastination at all costs. The procrastinator's self-esteem and inner serenity suffer as a result, and it frequently results in guilt, anxiety, self-loathing, or even melancholy. This price is much too expensive to bear.

The greatest remedy, as I've already stated, is to simply START. Do it now. Starting is the key to defeating procrastination. It's amazing how quickly starting your activity can shift your brain from procrastination mode to productivity.

Keep a tight eye on yourself whenever you employ one of the following justifications! You might be putting things off:

"I'm too exhausted," (Simply start. "I don't have time for that right now. You won't be weary in five minutes." "I need a break," you say (you do). (Stop for 5 minutes, then continue) "I don't feel like doing that right now; I'll feel like it tomorrow." (Just begin) "I'll start this tomorrow first thing; it's too late to start today." (Start now)

• "I've got too much on my plate." Consider your priorities.

• "I'm not sure where to start" It's not ideal (only to get started). (It never will be. Start) • "This is not the appropriate time," "I'm awaiting the appropriate time" (The right moment is always NOW)

Here are some suggestions on how to stop putting things off:

Solutions:

• Be 100 percent sincere with yourself. If you are inclined to put off a chore, consider the cost to yourself by delaying it.

• Jump right in (Action is the best antidote to procrastination).

• Pay attention to the outcomes you'll achieve by doing the activity you're inclined to put off.

- Concentrate on the benefits.

Work collaboratively (Coach, Accountability partner).

- Set deadlines for yourself.
- Break down work into manageable chunks.
- Finish the hardest task first thing in the morning.
- Pay attention to the work that generates revenue.

Don't begin next week or tomorrow! START NOW!

PLANNING AND SCHEDULING

You've probably heard wise sayings like the ones below.

"You can complete everything twice as quickly if you spend half as much time planning!"

"You can end up anyplace if you don't know where you are going," the saying goes.

"It won't get done if it's not on the calendar."

Perhaps you have mocked them or scoffed at them, saying things like, "But that's sooo apparent," "Nothing new," or "Common sense," and then you have returned to your stressful life without taking the time to hope for a miraculous transformation in the future.

As insignificant as those words may seem, they have the power to alter your course in life. Do you have a daily schedule? Or do you go through life doing the same things every day, addressing problems as they arise, putting out fires, etc.? Planning regularly alone can definitely drastically transform your life.

Setting the proper priorities and organising your vital job will be made easier for you if you plan your days, weeks, and even months in advance. Planning your week in advance on Sunday afternoon and "planning tomorrow today" is the best course of action.

List your tasks. Put all of your upcoming projects there, and give each one a due date and time. Keep the list visible and accessible at all times. You'll find it easier to focus all day if you do this. Work in blocks of time is an additional smart move. When I'm in the zone, I might work in three-hour blocks with a two-hour break in between, or I might work in 90-minute blocks with a 30-minute break in between.

Determine the three tasks that are most important for you to complete tomorrow. Don't forget to arrange leisure time, fun activities, and travel time as well as a little buffer for unexpected events.

Make time to begin your planning. When estimating how long a task will take, be realistic. Usually, I give myself an extra two hours. As a result, if I estimate that something will take an hour, I schedule two hours for it. As a result, I always have more time than I require because I consistently complete my assignments on time. The psychological impact of having accomplished things sooner and received rewards and feelings of wellbeing comes along with it. I hardly ever show signs of stress. The reverse occurs for the majority of people. If you are overly optimistic about the amount of time you have available, any work that takes longer than you anticipated will cause you to "lose" time, which will lower your mood. a persistent belief that you are failing to accomplish tasks, which eventually undermines your self-esteem.

I set goals for the coming year, quarters, months, weeks, and days, but I also allow myself the flexibility to alter these goals. You are in control. You can decide not to follow the plan or to come up with a fresh one. Planning offers you structure and direction, and that's what matters.

It's crucial to schedule your activities on your calendar. "If it's not on the calendar, it won't get done," always keep in mind.

Check your calendar every evening to view your objectives and plans for the following days. This will prevent you from wasting valuable time trying to figure out what to accomplish the following day, allowing you to start working right away.

Make plans now. The benefits are fantastic.

MINIMIZE DISTRACTIONS

You will likely feel the urge to remove more distractions after the clutter is gone (clutter is a type of visual distraction) and you are well on your way to becoming a minimalist.

Keep in mind that the more possessions you have, the more time they steal from you because you are constantly organising, cleaning, or moving things about.

Many people I know believe they are too busy, put in a lot of overtime, and don't know where or how to get free time.

When we take a closer look at their daily routine, we see that they check their email every 20 minutes, receive notifications from users who have seen their content on

Facebook or Twitter, and check each new email that arrives every 5 minutes. In addition to this, they are browsing the internet and seeing cat videos on Facebook and YouTube.

The capacity to stay focused is what separates successful people from failed ones.

The Approach:

- Shut down your web browser.
- Change the caller ID on your phone or unhook it.
- Shut off or at least silence your phone's sound and notification sounds. (I typically switch my phone to aeroplane mode to work efficiently and free of distractions.)
- End the email. Don't frequently check your email. (Twice daily for 30 minutes should suffice.)
- Log off all social media accounts.
- Establish regular times to check Facebook, Twitter, etc., and adhere to them.
- Lock the door to your workplace.

When you do some of these tasks, you'll have an hour or two free of text and phone-related interruptions. Try it!

You'll adore it as soon as you begin. You'll observe that you complete more tasks than before. Your productivity can increase dramatically with just one or two hours per day.

When working from home, be very careful about who you let to distract you. At the end of the month, when you wish you could get back the hours you wasted getting sidetracked and failing to complete the necessary tasks, the person who wants to go for coffee with you or take you to the mall most likely won't be paying your bills.

Don't switch on the television is yet another bit of advise. You are aware of it. Once it's on, your productivity is lost.

However, you can use the TV to your advantage by telling yourself, "If I finish what I set out to do today, I'll treat myself to one of my favourite shows."

THE 80/20 RULE

Vilfredo Pareto is my favourite. You cannot even begin to understand how much better my life is because of his philosophy.

This could be one of the most crucial chapters in the entire book for productivity, minimalism, and time management.

The fact that 20% of the Italian population held 80% of the land served as the foundation for Pareto's principle at the start of the 20th century. I employed Pareto's principle to reduce clutter and increase productivity, despite the fact that I initially questioned it because today it's more like 1 percent own 99 percent.

In his garden, where 80% of his tomatoes were produced by 20% of his tomato plants, Pareto discovered this ratio while conducting research on it. All is well thus far.

When wise people applied Pareto's law to business, they discovered the following:

20 percent of your actions will produce 80 percent of your results.

20 percent of your clientele generate 80% of your revenue.

20% of your clients are the source of 80% of your complaints.

20 percent of your products account for 80% of your sales.

20 percent of your clientele account for 80% of your sales.

If you can focus on the tasks that generate the most revenue while requiring the least amount of time, your business—and your free time—may expand dramatically.

That is unquestionably true in my line of work.

Twenty percent of my products provide 80% of my revenue.

20 percent of my advertisements generate 80 percent of my sales.

20% of my advertisements consume 80% of my budget.

so forth. . . It's incredible.

My success began when I focused on what generated 80% of my revenue (books), and then 80% of my time was devoted to that (writing, producing, and promoting books)

Regarding minimalism:

I saw that I spend 80% of my time in 20% of my home (that helped me with my decision to move onto a boat).

I discovered I only wore 20% of my T-shirts (I used to have 50 T-shirts, but now I only have 18, and guess what? I only wear the same six or seven).

same with pants and other clothing

I think you experience the same thing. Of course, correct me if I'm incorrect. This would imply that if you are as committed as I am, 80 percent of your wardrobe can be donated, or at least 40 percent if you want to proceed more slowly.

The 80:20 guideline may be found everywhere, even in your documents, bathroom, kitchen, and cupboard. I would wager on it if I could.

So, utilising Pareto's Principle, sit down and make a list of everything in your home, office, and place of business. Utilize the 80/20 rule in all facets of your personal and professional life. Later on, you can thank me.

TURN OFF YOUR PHONE

expressing the need for less possessions. How about receiving fewer calls, or more accurately, having your phone steal less of your time. Do you always pick up the phone? Well . . . don't! Let it occasionally go to voicemail. Your phone should be put away and turned off. Can't you? Do you think you'll lose the client? Yeah. I frequently heard that one. Essentially, from everyone I advised to do this. However, it never did. Leave a polite voicemail message that includes the standard "Sorry I'm busy and can't take your call right now." I'll give you a call as soon as I can.

Of course, your circumstances may differ, so you get to make the choice. I don't want you to lose your job because you don't return calls. Yet you understand what I mean. When you can, let the phone go to voicemail more frequently. If it's a crucial call, they'll call back.

Alternatively, they'll leave a message. Or you can call them if you see their phone number on your display. The only thing that is truly horrible is forgetting them or not calling them back as soon as you are done with what you are doing.

You save a tonne of time by not answering the phone every time it rings, along with all the advantages that come with it, such as increased productivity, more time for introspection, and more pleasure. Test it out.

Let's name him Steve. He was an extremely stressed-out sales manager who came to me on the verge of serious burnout. He received 60 to 80 calls each day and was constantly on the phone putting out fires and trying to solve everyone's concerns, which left him with no time to accomplish his true job, which was to market his goods and visit clients. He was worried that he would lose clients, which would affect his ability to keep his career, but he was on the verge of a breakdown so he tried it. He made the decision to alter his voice mail's message and to let calls go to voice mail for at least an hour each day. "Hi. I'm now unable to access the phone. When I can, I'll give you a call again. Send me a WhatsApp message if it's urgent, that's all.

The first two weeks saw nothing. By the time he returned calls in the third week, 80% of the issues that people had first contacted about had been resolved. Suddenly, he was receiving barely half as many calls. He had no urgent WhatsApp messages, either. A month later, he felt at ease. He reasoned that there may have been fewer calls because vacation time was approaching or business was slow. He finally had to accept it to himself three months later! His time was within his control. Because he wasn't always thinking about work, he had more time to plan interesting activities to do with his family during his leisure time on weekends.

He continued to exceed corporate sales records for a few years before joining the sales team of a rival company that treated him much better than his former boss. All this, nine months after making the decision to not pick up the phone whenever it rang. Magical.

TURN OFF YOUR TV

Simplify everything. Turning off your TV will be a major game changer.

According to studies, the average American and European both watch TV for 4 to 5 hours per day. Younger generations most likely watch less television, but they are still attracted to their screens, whether it be Netflix, Disney+, HBO Max, YouTube, or social media.

This indicates that the typical person watches between 28 and 35 hours of TV (or any of the above) each week.

The greatest energy consumer, if not the biggest, is television. It maintains your trance. Do you ever feel revitalised or revived after watching TV—aside from, of course, after witnessing an outstanding motivational speech?

Unless you utilise TV to watch things that can truly help you, it is a source of negativity and junk and won't be of any assistance to you. I attribute the widespread terror we experienced over the past two years to television.

Don't get me wrong. The pandemic happened. But if the media kept track of every sickness or car accident death, we wouldn't be able to leave the house anymore. Have you ever noticed that the counter resets to zero each year for all the other illnesses? deaths from drugs, the flu, and cancer. The counter resets to zero at the end of the year. The COVID alone keeps growing. I'm curious as to why that is.

Anyways. Turn off the TV and take use of the extra time you have to go on walks, read good books, spend more time with loved ones and friends, go to the gym, have more fun, and much more. TV is heavily slanted to only show us the negative tales.

Start carefully and reduce your TV viewing if you are truly dependent on your box (although I recommend you go cold turkey). Just put it to the test! See how you feel after a week without watching TV.

Not to worry. The crucial information will still remain current because your friends, family, and coworkers will keep you informed. Just pick and choose what you expose your mind to, and be discriminating. According to several research, those who don't watch TV are actually better reality judges than those who do.

Read one of the great books about how the media sways us and how almost everything is fake if you need more motivation to stop watching television. You may choose what information you are exposed to. Ensure that it enhances your life. Watch a documentary or a comedy instead of trash TV. Consider listening to an audiobook or motivational CD in your car instead of the news.

I've had the following encounters with the media:

• Wednesday-recorded radio shows that are offered as "live" on Sunday. Until Sunday, I was unable to talk about it or share it on social media.

When I was a guest on a talk show, I received the questions one day in advance so I could prepare myself extremely well. A well-known radio presenter read the entire show from a script that other people produced for him. Great speeches from the anchor read from a teleprompter.

Stop watching TV and appreciate the advantages of living simply.

WHAT'S THE MOST IMPORTANT THING?

Decide on priorities. What holds the biggest significance? Every morning, start with this. If you do the three most crucial things every day, I bet you can achieve extraordinary and unthinkable development.

Yup. I've said enough. You will be in an entirely different—and significantly better—position if you perform the three tasks that are most crucial to your life every day for a full year. Finding out what these three things are every day is the challenging part.

Make a list of your top priorities now and before you go to sleep each night. why just before bed? Since your subconscious mind will then work on it while you sleep, you'll be focused, know exactly what to do, and be ready to start working as soon as you wake up the following day. Sounds absurd? Try it. You will be shocked.

The only way to find time is to be aware of your priorities. Priorities are always important. The phrase "Oh, I don't have time" is never used when I speak with other coaches. This is so that we may say, "You are not as essential to me as this other item," knowing that the other person will understand. And it's alright. Such is life.

You will never be able to do everything you need to do in a single day. There will never be a time when you can put things off until "when I have time." Priorities and options are key. It's best if you obtain it as soon as possible. The exciting part is that if you start prioritising and choosing, you will eventually have enough time.

What, then, do you currently consider to be most important?

ME TIME

You have more time when you own less stuff. Less clothing is washed and ironed more quickly (I don't even iron, so I save even more time). Less junk gets put away more quickly. What follows, then? There will be more time. I strongly advise you to set aside some of that time for "Me-time." time that is just for you. You can use it to read a nice book, practise meditation, list five things for which you are grateful, or simply do anything you choose. This is quite significant. In the long run, it will soothe your anxiety and make you happier. Me-time is a huge part of self-care, which is incredibly important.

You have more time to listen to yourself when the useless items leave your home or flat. You'll be able to concentrate and reason. You'll cease flitting from one urgency to the next like a bird without a head.

If you choose minimalism as a lifestyle, there won't be as many lengthy, demanding, stressful days, but there will be significantly fewer.

Make the most of the extra time by turning a large portion of it into "Me time." Valuing your time has a special quality. You'll have more time if you value your time more because other people will value it more as well.

GET RID OF INTERRUPTIONS

How frequently are you called out during the day? No matter how many hours you put in, you won't be able to do quality work if you let people interrupt you. Because it takes your brain 7 to 25 minutes to regain focus after a 5-minute break, studies show that you lose 12 to 32 minutes for every interruption at work. How frequently are you interrupted each day? 10? 12? How much time can you save if the interruptions are fewer? How? Decide in advance when interruptions are permitted. Make it clear when people can call you, for instance, or put your phone on aeroplane mode for three hours and you'll be more productive since you'll be laser-focused. Turn off your emails and notifications, and don't even attempt to multitask because doing so will only make you more stupid.

According to a University of London study, checking your email while working intently is equivalent to deducting 10 points from your IQ. A TEN-POINTER!

That has the same impact as going without sleep for 36 hours. Have you ever worked after a 36-hour sleepless period? How did that turn out? I suppose not very well. A side note: Marijuana use only lowers IQ by 4 points.

When you work in a corporate office, it can be challenging to put this into practise, but it is possible. Nothing will occur if you switch off your email for two to three hours or your phone for the same amount of time (unless you are an ambulance driver or a doctor).

Make it obvious when you are available and when you are not in case your coworkers or perhaps your supervisor disturb you. Find a method for people to contact you in an emergency and follow the same procedures for emails and phone calls (WhatsApp, special email address, etc.)

If coworkers or your supervisor don't agree with you on the value of uninterrupted work, give them a copy of one of my other books, such as The Productivity Revolution or

Destination Happiness, or suggest having me speak at your organisation.

Additionally, you may send them a photo of this chapter. Even if they do have time, people typically dislike time management techniques. because the truth can be painful and this is the harsh truth. Your life will improve if you are willing to endure the discomfort and apply the advice.

I swear.

SAY "NO" AND SAY IT OFTEN

Minimalists reject many things and do so frequently. When you start decluttering, you say "NO" to a lot of stuff that don't belong in your closet, bedroom, living room, or other places. You will eventually refuse highly emotional things, as well as people and professional ties. And that's alright since your life will get better with time.

You're really saying yes to your new YOU and your new way of life when you learn to say "NO" and stop trying to please everyone else.

Freedom and sincerity start when a "No" is a "No" rather than a "Yes" that is said only to appease others. The "Yes" gains strength, sincerity, awareness, and commitment, increasing its value.

Gain the confidence to decline invitations. You'll say "No" a lot during the decluttering process since you'll be saying it a lot. Once you start turning folks down, you can choose whether or not to clarify that it's nothing personal. You have the choice. Nobody is entitled to an explanation or defence from you.

That may sound a little self-centered, though. It is, too! However, never forget who is most significant in your life. That is correct! The most significant person in your life is YOU. You need to be healthy. Only after you are in good health can you be in good health toward others. From this level, you can help others, but only after you are in good health.

People who are happy, successful, and productive tend to use the word "NO" a lot. Minimalists use the word "NO" a lot. Any patterns here?

Beginning to say "NO" will make life much better for you! You are well on your way to being a Minimalist if you start doing it on a regular basis.

CONCLUSION

We are here! The book is already nearing its conclusion. Wasn't that quick, though? Have you already started decluttering, or did you only skim the book and plan to reread it and put its advice into practise later?

It's a good thing I began decluttering in 2016 or 2017. Just look at how far I've come. The wonderful thing is that, if I can accomplish it, so can you. Maybe in a different way—YOUR WAY—but I'm confident you'll be able to take use of its advantages.

The Happy Minimalist's title and subtitle were fairly audacious on my part. How to live a life that is easier, more organised, and happier while also finding inner peace. All those promises are a lot. I hope I lived up to or, at the very least, surpassed your expectations. The path to minimalism should lead to a reduction in stress and a rise in happiness. These are the "side affects" I personally have encountered, as have all minimalists I have come across or read about.

You must, of course, put in the effort. A word of caution: just because you're happier and less stressed doesn't mean that your life will no longer be filled with tension, despair, and unhappiness. They will occasionally appear because they are a part of life, but you will be able to handle them better.

Ah. I have some book suggestions I owe you. The books listed below are the ones that guided me the most:

- Marie Kondo, The Magic of Tidying Up
- Condense — Joshua Becker
- Karen Kingston, "Clear your Clutter with Feng Shui"
- 10-Minute Declutter — Barrie Davenport and S.J. Scott
- The Minimalists, or minimalism

Greg McKeown on essentialism

What? Six novels, only? Yes. Actually, ONE is sufficient. Keep in mind that starting to do is more crucial than simply reading numerous books on simplicity. So, I'm assuming you've already begun your minimalistic adventure.

All the best!

Marc

CPSIA information can be obtained
at www.ICGtesting.com
Printed in the USA
LVHW081815261122
734044LV00013B/495

9 781944 237196